CQ's Legislative Simulation

CQ's Legislative Simulation

Government in Action

Julie Dolan
Macalester College

and

Marni Ezra
Hood College

CQ PRESS

A Division of Congressional Quarterly Inc.
Washington, D.C.

CQ Press
A Division of Congressional Quarterly Inc.
1255 22nd Street, N.W., Suite 400
Washington, D.C. 20037

202-822-1475; 800-638-1710

www.cqpress.com

⊗ The paper used in this publication meets the minimum requirements of the American National Standard for Information Sciences—Permanence of Paper for Printed Library Materials, ANSI Z39.48-1992.

Cover and interior designs: Karen Doody

Printed and bound in the United States of America

05 04 03 02 01   5 4 3 2 1

Library of Congress Cataloging-in-Publication Data

Dolan, Julie.
    CQ's legislative simulation : government in action / Julie Dolan and Marni Ezra.
       p. cm. – (Government in action)
    Includes bibliographical references and index.
    ISBN 1-56802-709-5 (p. : alk. paper)
    1. Legislation—Political aspects—United States.   I. Ezra, Marni, 1969–   II. Title.

KF4945 .D65 2001
328.73'077—dc21

                                                                        2001043581

To Bill

—J. D.

To David, Sam, and Zoey

—M. E.

Contents

Foreword

CQ Press is pleased to introduce a new line of educational tools designed to incorporate traditionally researched topics into a learning environment. The long-awaited Government in Action series offers firsthand experience on the workings of the government. Whether read in the library by patrons interested in learning about the government or used in the classroom by students and instructors, the Government in Action series is a rich classroom-tested tool that will benefit anyone seeking to gain a better understanding of how our democracy works. Volumes in the series include *CQ's Legislative Simulation: Government in Action, CQ's White House Media Simulation: Government in Action, CQ's Congressional Election Simulation: Government in Action,* and *CQ's Supreme Court Simulation: Government in Action.*

Resources Available on the Web

Several free resources to enhance and update this simulation are available at http://www.cqpress.com/library/gia, including

- an instructor's manual on how to conduct a classroom simulation
- updates for the current Congress, including standing committees and committee rosters
- overviews of roles, responsibilities, exercises, and assignments
- witness testimonies, a questionnaire on members of Congress, and other tips and suggestions

Whether encouraging library research or facilitating classroom simulations, the Government in Action series is an ideal reference tool. We are very interested in your impression of our new series, and we encourage you to send your feedback to gia@cqpress.com.

CQ Press

Preface

When we began teaching courses on the U.S. legislative process, we used a simulation that came with the popular text *Congress and Its Members,* by Roger H. Davidson and Walter J. Oleszek. We are grateful to them and their colleague Robert Tennant for creating the simulation on which our book is based. Our students have benefited greatly from playing the roles of U.S. House members, and we have many good memories of the different casts of characters that have come through our classes over the years.

Since first using the legislative simulation, we have continually updated the content and, in the process, changed the legislation, added materials, updated and enlarged the text, and created new manuals for both participants and leaders. Because our colleagues continue to request our updated simulation, we decided to create a new version of the original one by Davidson, Oleszek, and Tennant. Over and over, our teaching evaluations have shown that students both enjoy and learn a great deal from this simulation. Thus we hope that through its publication this simulation will reach a wider audience of instructors, librarians, and students.

This book is divided into two parts. Part I consists of two chapters. Chapter 1 is a primer on the legislative process in the U.S. House of Representatives. We suggest that participants read this chapter before starting the simulation. Chapter 2, a guide to the simulation itself, walks participants step by step through the structure of the simulation and their roles and responsibilities in it. Part II contains the supporting materials that participants will need to play their roles in the simulation. Included are the texts of the legislation that will be debated, lists of the committee members and witnesses who will discuss each bill, and background articles on the bills and the issues they address. Participants will find witness testimonies on the Web at http://library.cqpress.com/gia. Although each participant will need to use outside sources to research his or her own member of Congress, all of the information about the issue under consideration is included in Part II.

Acknowledgments

Many people gave us their helpful comments and support in getting this book published. First, we would like to thank our editor at CQ Press, Adrian Forman, for overseeing this project from beginning to end. Further thanks go to our manuscript editor, Sabra Ledent, for her remarkable attention to detail throughout the editing process. We also would like to thank our colleagues Melissa Deckman and Michele Swers, who offered many useful suggestions. Another colleague, Susan Webb Hammond, piloted the simulation in her legislative process class at American University. We are indebted to her for all of her insightful suggestions and guidance. In addition, we are grateful to our student assistants, Yana Sokolenko and Andrew Kish, who reviewed the manuscript and provided us with valuable comments. Finally, we would like to thank our colleagues and mentors at American University, who taught us the love of teaching Congress as well as the value of experiential learning.

Julie Dolan
Marni Ezra

A Legislative Primer

CHAPTER 1

The Legislative Process of the U.S. House of Representatives

The House of Representatives is a complex legislative institution that was designed by the Founders to be the "people's branch" of the federal Congress. Until 1913, only House members were directly elected by the people; their counterparts in the Senate were elected by the state legislatures. The Seventeenth Amendment erased this distinction between the two branches by providing for popular election of senators. In keeping with the notion of direct representation on which the House was founded, the country is divided into geographical districts of roughly equal population, and each district is allotted one House representative to do its bidding in Washington.

The U.S. Constitution stipulates that House members must face reelection every two years. The voters, then, have ample opportunity to throw members out of office should they stray too far from their constituents' desires. Keeping in mind their short term, members of the House stay well tuned to voters' concerns.

The two main jobs of members of Congress are to represent their constituents and to pass legislation. These two tasks, which are dependent on each other, often come into conflict, forcing legislators to choose between satisfying their constituents, their own conscience, their party, their state, their delegation, their region, and, perhaps, their president. In order to represent their constituents, members of Congress must pass or block legislation that will help or harm their districts. Yet in order to pass legislation that is good for the nation they must sometimes forsake the very same constituents who put them in office.

A couple of examples illustrate this point. Elected as a Democrat in 1992 to the Thirteenth Congressional District in Pennsylvania, a district that had elected Republicans for the previous seventy-six years, newcomer Marjorie Margolis-Mezvinsky faced a daunting challenge during her first year in Congress. That year, President Bill Clinton's deficit reduction plan, the first crucial piece of legislation debated in his presidency, came up for a vote. The president's budget plan had already passed the Senate by one vote, with Vice President Al Gore casting the deciding vote. In the House, the Clinton team needed one more vote to pass the bill and the responsibility for that final vote fell on Margolis-Mezvinsky. As part of her 1992 election campaign, Margolis-Mezvinsky had promised her constituents that she would not raise their taxes, but, unfortunately for her, Clinton's deficit reduction package did just that. If she voted for the bill she would break her promise to her constituents and was certain to lose her bid for reelection the next year. If she voted against the bill she was turning her back on her party, her president, and what she felt was best for the nation. In the end, Margolis-Mezvinsky chose to vote with the president. Predictably, she was not reelected in 1994.

More recently, Republican James Rogan was elected in 1996 to represent the people of the Twenty-seventh Congressional District of California. In this district, which is home to NBC Studios, Disney headquarters, and a variety of smaller entertainment businesses,[1] Democrats outnumbered Republicans by about 44 percent to 37 percent and were generally favorable toward President Clinton.[2] The district favored Clinton by an eight-percentage-point margin in both the 1992 and 1996 elections. In 1998, Rogan, who served on the House Judiciary Committee, played an active role in the impeachment proceedings against President Clinton. He even served as one of the House impeachment managers. As the impeachment proceedings unfolded, Rogan became one of the most vocal critics of Clinton, advocating the president's removal from office. In the 2000 elections, Rogan was challenged for his seat by Democrat Adam Schiff who claimed that Rogan was "an extremist out of touch with his district."[3] During the race, Rogan acknowledged that his impeachment activities may have cost him precious votes, explaining, "If I lose this race it will be because of impeachment. I used to draw Democrats and independents. They liked me . . . but those people supported Clinton. And they'll never support me now." [4] The election only confirmed his prediction; Schiff defeated Rogan by eight percentage points, leading political observers to conclude that being out of step with his constituents on the impeachment matter sealed Rogan's electoral fate.[5]

These two examples of members of Congress behaving contrary to their constituents' wishes and subsequently being defeated for reelection illustrate an important lesson about lawmaking in the House of Representatives. At times, the wishes of a legislator's district and political party work together, making that legislator's decision easier. For example, on January 3, 2001, Democratic member of Congress James Traficant of Ohio sponsored H.R. 222, which, if passed, would increase the hourly minimum wage by $1 over two years. Because the largest industry in Traficant's district is automobile manufacturing and his district has a strong union presence, his district and his party pushed him to support legislation that helps workers. On many issues, however, the desires of a legislator's district and political party clash and create tough choices for him or her. These tensions do not emerge for all pieces of legislation, only those particularly important to a legislator's constituency or where the will of the constituency and another influence on the legislator come into conflict.

Passing bills and resolutions is the main goal of the legislative process. Although legislators must keep the will of their constituents in mind, they also must concentrate on crafting legislation that can gain the support of the majority of their colleagues. The complexities and breadth of the legislation brought before Congress reflect the extraordinary diversity of the nation itself. Just contemplate the diversity of interests represented by the fifty states, which stretch from Hawaii to Maine and from Florida to Alaska. The needs of these states and their people have common threads, but the differences are immense. Moreover, legislation does not affect all areas of the nation equally. For example, the North American Free Trade Agreement (NAFTA), which opened up trade between the United States, Mexico, and Canada, was met with hostile opposition from citizens in states that would be directly and adversely affected, but was applauded by others around the nation as a good policy for the United States. Whether or not a legislator's constituents will be harmed economically is often central to the legislator's decision to support or oppose a piece of legislation. For NAFTA, many members of Congress who believed their

constituents would be harmed by the legislation, such as Democrats John Dingell and John Conyers Jr. of Michigan, voted against the bill. With auto manufacturers in their districts, both feared NAFTA would cost much-needed jobs back home.

Introducing Legislation

To become law, proposed legislation must be approved in identical form by both the House and the Senate and then signed by the president. Legislative proposals usually follow parallel paths through the two chambers of Congress.

Bills emerge from many sources. Members themselves, aided by their staffs, develop a large share of proposals; contacts with constituents often help members identify problems requiring legislative solutions. The actual drafting may be undertaken by committee and subcommittee staffs or the offices of legislative counsel—the lawyers in both the House and the Senate who specialize in drafting bills. A bill can go through many drafts before a satisfactory version is produced.

Another source of legislation is the executive branch. Most presidents come into office with an extensive legislative agenda that takes the form of a flood of bills from the White House to Capitol Hill. Typically, modern presidents are most successful legislatively in the first portion of their four-year term of office. This "honeymoon" period is associated with the president's generally high standing with the public immediately after the election.

Lobbyists are yet another source of legislation. Congressional support agencies such as the General Accounting Office, the Congressional Budget Office, and the Congressional Research Service of the Library of Congress provide members and committees with ideas and language for bills or resolutions.

During this initial stage of the legislative process, members may ask colleagues to join them in introducing a bill. The advantage of cosponsorship is broad-based support toward passage of the legislation; the downside is that cosponsors may demand modifications in the proposal that correspond to their own interests as the price for their support.

The sponsor or sponsors of legislation introduce their bill by placing it in the "hopper," a wire basket located at the lower left-hand corner of the Speaker's rostrum in the House chamber. The Speaker is both the presiding officer of the House and the overall leader of the major party in the chamber. The bill is accepted by the bill clerk, an employee of the House. The House parliamentarian, another House employee, assigns the bill a number and directs it (at least the more noncontroversial bills) to the appropriate committee of jurisdiction. Formally, bills are referred to committee by the Speaker, but, in practice, referral decisions are almost always made by the parliamentarian on the Speaker's behalf.

The Speaker of the House has many options when referring a bill to committee. Although the House rules spell out jurisdictions for assigning bills to the chamber's standing committees (see next section), often more than one committee will have a claim to jurisdiction over a bill. If the Speaker supports a bill,[6] he may refer it to a committee that is friendly toward passage. But if he wants to defeat the legislation, he may refer it to an antagonistic committee or several committees in an attempt to kill it.

Navigating the Committee System

If each member of Congress had to research and deal with the thousands of items that arise every year, Congress could not finish its work. Committees, therefore, represent a division of labor. By allocating the work of the institution to different committees, members are able to become experts in the areas important to their constituents and to themselves. Those who are already experts can help to create better legislation.

Both the House and Senate are divided into standing committees that review almost all legislation and determine whether it will be considered by the entire chamber. In the 107th Congress (2001–2002) the House of Representatives has nineteen standing committees that range in size from nine to seventy-five members (see box "Standing Committees, House of Representatives, 107th Congress").

Each committee in Congress is composed of members of both the majority and minority parties. The membership of most committees is determined by the proportion of seats that the Democrats and Republicans control in the chamber. But because the majority party sets the rules, it can decide to give itself more than its fair share of committee seats. For example, in the 1998 elections to the 106th Congress Democrats gained five seats in the House (from 205 to 210), yet the mix of the number of Republicans and Democrats sitting on each committee remained relatively unaltered from the 105th Congress. Republicans controlled 51 percent of the seats in the House but 54.9 percent of all committee seats, a difference of thirty seats that Democrats claimed should have been theirs.[7] The majority party is especially prone to exceed its fair share of members on the most important committees, such as

> ### STANDING COMMITTEES, HOUSE OF REPRESENTATIVES, 107TH CONGRESS
>
> Agriculture
> Appropriations
> Armed Services
> Budget
> Education and the Workforce
> Energy and Commerce
> Financial Services
> Government Reform
> House Administration
> International Relations
> Judiciary
> Resources
> Rules
> Science
> Small Business
> Standards of Official Conduct
> Transportation and Infrastructure
> Veterans' Affairs
> Ways and Means

Rules, Ways and Means, and Appropriations, because the decisions of these committees on proposed bills are typically crucial to the majority party's legislative agenda.

Standing committees are further divided into subcommittees, or "mini-committees," which allows members to specialize even further. In the House, legislation is typically referred from the full committee to a subcommittee where most of the legislative work is done. On average, each committee has five subcommittees. Indeed, House rules passed in 1995 and revised in 2001 stipulate that no committee may have more than five subcommittees except for Appropriations (which has thirteen), Government Reform (eight), International Relations (six), and Transportation and Infrastructure (six). Any other committee that provides oversight (that is, reviews federal agencies and government programs and performance), may not have more than six subcommittees.

Once the committee jurisdiction has been determined, the bill is sent physically to the committee or committees. Each committee chair and staff have the option of doing nothing with the bill, but if action is deemed appropriate, the staff schedule hearings and announce the committee's plans to other legislators, lobbyists, and the press.

Committee Hearings

Committee hearings are an extremely important step in the legislative process. It is at this stage that members learn about legislation, ask questions of experts, and determine others' positions on legislation. In this open process, interest groups, members of the executive branch, academics and experts, and even ordinary citizens can testify about a piece of legislation. Although committee hearings are almost always open to the public, a committee may elect to close its hearing to the public if a majority of members of the committee agree to do so for national security reasons.[8] Committees often post their hearing schedules on their Web sites. These schedules also appear in the major national newspapers and are frequently broadcast on C-SPAN.[9]

Hearings are conducted by the committee or subcommittee chair, unless he or she relinquishes the gavel to a colleague (usually of the majority party) while attending to other duties. In the first stage of a committee hearing the committee chair and ranking minority member (usually the most senior committee member of the minority party) make opening remarks outlining their views of the bill and the direction they would like to see the bill take. The chair also usually thanks the witnesses who have agreed to testify. If other members of the committee make opening remarks, they usually speak in order of seniority, beginning with the most senior members.

After the committee members' opening remarks, the witnesses offer their testimony. Current House rules require witnesses to "file with the committee [at least X hours] in advance of the appearance a written statement of proposed testimony and . . . limit the oral presentation to the Committee to brief summary thereof." [10] This way, members and their staffs have time to study the advance copies of the testimony and prepare questions for the witnesses. Some committees allow witnesses only five minutes in which to summarize orally their written testimony.[11] Thus witnesses usually provide a short statement summarizing their position on the bill and the reasons they support, oppose, or would like to change the proposed legislation. Both oral and written testimonies become part of the public record.

Typically, the first witnesses to testify are from the executive branch and are referred to as "administration witnesses." They may indicate whether the president is likely to sign or veto the bill and propose changes to the legislation that could lead to presidential support. For example, when the House was considering new gun control legislation after the 1999 massacre at Colorado's Columbine High School, U.S. Deputy Attorney General Eric Holder Jr., representing the U.S. Justice Department, appeared before the House Judiciary Committee to speak in favor of the president's initiative for reducing gun violence. If the committee encounters resistance from the administration, the legislation's path is bumpier than it might have been, but success is not impossible.

Administration witnesses are followed by "public witnesses," members of the public such as academics, experts, and interest group representatives. Some committees hear proponents and opponents on alternating days or half-days. Sometimes panels of like-minded supporting or opposing witnesses testify in order to make presentations more concise and interesting for members.

After the witnesses have presented their views, they are questioned by committee members. The chair begins the questioning, followed by the ranking minority party member, and then other committee members in order (Republican, Democrat) until everyone has had an opportunity to speak. If there is time left over, the chair may divide it among those members who have further questions. Exchanges between committee members and witnesses are included in the verbatim record of the hearing and become part of the legislative history of the bill being considered. For example, if a committee member learns from a witness that the measure would do something radically different from the intended outcome, the member might then seek to amend the measure during the markup session (described later in this chapter) and would use the information gleaned from the hearings to provide the rationale for doing so. If that amendment later became part of the legislation, anyone wishing to know the origin of the amendment, and especially the government agencies that have to actually implement the legislation, could consult the record of the hearing.

Hearings can serve other purposes as well. Most important, they can be used to showcase an issue. Indeed, interest groups often ask a celebrity to present their views before a committee, because such witnesses can generate intense media attention for an issue and increase the pressure on legislators to act. Actors are favorite invitees—such as Charlton Heston for the National Rifle Association and Michael J. Fox in behalf of research on Parkinson's disease. And legislators themselves may encourage sensational or poignant testimony to produce media attention. Hearings also can serve to increase a member's visibility, which is especially important for those interested in pursuing other offices or hoping simply to further their reelection prospects. Finally, members can use hearings as an opportunity to establish their positions on the issues through their statements and questioning of witnesses. These members may be seeking to shore up support from constituents or important interest groups.

The relationship between the committee chair and the ranking member has an important influence on the tone and success of the hearings. If the chair and ranking member work well together and run the committee in a bipartisan fashion, the hearings will typically produce information that is highly useful to members' decision making about the pending legislation. When party leaders clash and the committee is divided, witnesses are often treated in a more hostile fashion, and members ask questions as much to make a point as to learn new information.

Committee Markup

After the committee has completed its hearings, the bill is ready to be marked up (see box "Script of a Mock Committee Markup").[12] It is rare that a bill makes it to the floor of the House without first being changed by the committee to which it was originally referred. During markup, the committee goes through the bill line by line making additions or deletions, often drawing from witness testimony provided during committee hearings. Members may change the order of the text, the punctuation, the title of the bill, sections of the bill, or the entire text of the bill itself. Like committee hearings, markup sessions are usu-

---

SCRIPT OF A MOCK COMMITTEE MARKUP

Chairman: "The Committee is meeting today for consideration of the bill H.R. _____, a bill for the purposes of _____ ."

Chairman: "Does any Member have an opening statement?"

[Opening statements]

Chairman: "The clerk will read the bill."

[Clerk reads entire bill.]

Chairman: "The clerk will read section 1 of the bill."

[Clerk reads section 1.]

Chairman: "Are there any amendments to section 1 of the bill?"

Member X: "I have an amendment."

Chairman: "The clerk will read the amendment."

[Clerk reads the amendment in full.]

Chairman: "The gentleman is recognized in support of his amendment."

Member X: [Speaks in support of amendment for five minutes, or as much of the five minutes as he consumes.]

Chairman: "Do any other members wish to be heard on the amendment?"

[Other members speak on amendment under the five-minute rule: "Mr. Chairman, I move to strike the last word."]

Chairman: "The question occurs on the amendment of Member X. All in favor say aye . . . All opposed say no."

[Vote]

Chairman: "The ayes have it. The amendment is agreed to."

Chairman: "Are there any other amendments to section 1?"

Chairman: "The clerk will read section 2 of the bill."

[Clerk reads section 2 in full.]

[Repeat process above until all amendments completed.]

Member Y: "Mr. Chairman, I move that the bill H.R. _____ be reported favorably to the House with an amendment."

Chairman: "The question is on the motion. All in favor say aye . . . All opposed say no."

[Vote]

Chairman: "The motion is agreed to, and without objection the question of reconsideration is laid upon the table."

Member Y: "I move that, pursuant to clause 1 of rule XXII, the committee authorize the chairman to offer such motions as may be necessary in the House to go to conference with the Senate on the bill H.R. _____ or a similar Senate bill."

Chairman: "The question is on the motion. All in favor say aye . . . All opposed say no."

[Vote]

Chairman: "The motion is agreed to."

Member Z: "Pursuant to clause 2(l) of rule XI, I assert my right to two days for the purpose of filing additional views on the bill just ordered reported."

Chairman: "All members will have two days for the purpose of filing views."

Chairman: "Without objection, the committee now stands adjourned."

[If objection is heard, adjournment may be agreed to by motion.]

Source: U.S. House of Representatives, Committee on Rules, Majority Office.

ally open to the public, unless they deal with national security or other sensitive matters.

Members of Congress keep the interests of their constituents in mind throughout the markup session. They may delete portions of a bill that they deem harmful to their constituents or add provisions to a bill that may help their district. Committee chairs keep the bill moving and mediate disputes between members with different interests and concerns.

Several strategies are used at the markup stage of the legislative process. Proponents of a bill may attempt to broaden it, thereby giving the bill a better chance to succeed on the House floor. To win enough votes to get a bill through markup, chairs may accept amendments geared to specific members' interests. With district or state interests on the line, members may lobby their colleagues to support the bill, either in the committee or on the floor. Seeking a quite different result, opponents of a bill often try to add unnecessary amendments so the legislation will fail. Last-minute additions to a bill can slow the markup process and make the bill too complicated and confusing for easy disposition.

General Procedural Rules. Each committee determines the number of members needed (quorum) for committee proceedings to begin, but House rules require that a minimum of two committee members be present. At least one minority member must be on hand for any committee session, including markup sessions, to proceed. If during a committee proceeding a member seeks recognition for a point of order (that is, the member believes the rules of the group are being violated), that member must be recognized. The member must then state the point of order succinctly, and it must relate to a suspected violation of rules on which the chair must rule. Similarly, a member may seek to be recognized for a parliamentary inquiry, in which the member seeks to clarify the present status of debate, discussion, rights, or rules on which that member is not clear and is seeking advice or a ruling from the chair. This course is to be used for a genuine inquiry, not simply to make a statement or to otherwise pursue one's political or legislative goals. A member may be ruled out of order by the chair if the chair determines that the inquiring member does not seek to make a germane inquiry.[13]

After the Republicans took control of Congress in 1995, they used their new majority status to eliminate proxy voting, a procedure that allowed those members present in committee markup sessions (usually the committee chair) to vote the wishes of absent colleagues.[14]

Many members of Congress expressed their displeasure with this change of rule as they were forced to run from committee to committee and back to the floor of the chamber in order not to miss any votes. The elimination of proxy voting diminished the power of committee chairs because they could no longer speak for their colleagues, but it was expected to make members more accountable by requiring them to attend committee meetings in order to voice their concerns.

Markup Rules. Ground rules bring order to the consideration of bills. During markup, the committee chair has the discretion to render rulings on both technical and substantive questions. But, like for all rulings, any aggrieved member may appeal the chair's decisions, thereby opening the way for a vote by the full committee. Although committee members can challenge a ruling of the chair, they must remember that by winning such a battle, they may in the long run lose the war by finding their ability to function within the committee impaired. Thus members must calculate carefully before making such a challenge. Moreover, custom dictates that all majority party committee members vote to support the chair's rulings, especially if the challenge comes from the minority party.

The committee begins consideration of a bill in markup with the first title, or first section, and continues through the last title and last section. The committee may decide to make tentative decisions on amendments and then return to take final votes on each amendment or each title or each section. Members can agree to the procedure before they begin considering amendments.

Amendments. Any member of the committee can present an amendment to any title or section of a title of any legislation before the committee so long as the amendment is "germane" to the title or section to be amended. Amendments must be seconded, which means that one member proposes the amendment and a second member adds his or her support.

An amendment is considered germane if it properly relates to the legislation. If the amendment in question does not fall within the area of the legislation being considered, it is subject to a point of order of "nongermaneness" and can be stricken. Points of order may also be raised on the floor of the House if the subcommittee or committee allows nongermane amendments to accompany a bill. Whether an amendment is germane is determined by the committee chair, and that decision is subject to a vote, if called, by the full subcommittee or committee.

Reporting the Bill

After the committee has finished its markup, the committee chair calls for a vote on whether to send the bill to the full House chamber. If the committee votes to report out the bill, it has several choices on how to do so. First, though rare, it may report the bill out unchanged—that is, the text of the original bill introduced in the House remains intact. Second, it may report the bill out with one comprehensive amendment—called an amendment in the nature of a substitute—which strikes out all of the text after the enacting clause and substitutes the text of the amended bill.[15] Third, it may report the bill with a series of amendments. And, fourth, it may order a clean bill reported. A clean bill is the original bill along with the amendments adopted by the committee, all of which are reintroduced and assigned a new number.

A member wishing to report an amended bill would say, "Mr. Chairman (or Madam Chairman), I move that the committee report the bill _____ (as amended). Furthermore, I move to instruct the staff to prepare the legislative report, to make the technical and conforming amendments, and that the chairperson take all necessary steps to bring the bill before the House for consideration." A member wishing to introduce a clean bill would say, "Mr. Chairman (or Madam Chairman), I move that a clean bill be prepared by the chairman." The committee then votes on the motion, which requires a majority to pass.

Along with the approved marked-up bill, the committee provides the entire House with a report of the bill, which summarizes the substance of the bill as well as any changes made to the bill in committee. The report also provides the committee's rationale for changing the legislation and the votes of committee members. Dissenting views of members are included in the report as are the views of members who voted for the bill but who may have a rationale for their vote that differs from that of the rest of the committee. Once a bill is reported, it may be considered for debate on the floor of the House. For interest groups, members of the public, the media, and other members of Congress who did not sit on the committee meetings or were not able to attend any of the committee's proceedings, committee reports are an excellent source of detailed information about the pending legislation.

Floor Debate

Before certain bills are debated on the floor of the House, they are sent to the Rules Committee, which establishes the rules for debate. Only a small portion of bills receive a rule (about 10 percent), but these bills are usually the most important ones that Congress debates. Most routine, noncontroversial bills go to the floor under a suspension of the rules—that is, debate on the bill is limited to forty minutes and no amendments are allowed. Because these bills go to the floor under such a strict procedure, no rule is needed from the Rules Committee.

Three basic rules govern the floor debate:

Closed rule. A specified period of time for general debate is allowed on the bill, but no amendments are permitted.

Modified closed rule. Members who propose specific amendments to specific parts of the bill (other parts of the measure are closed to amendment) may be heard, and amendments may be debated on the floor after the specified general debate time is exhausted.

Open rule. Members may propose amendments to each title and its section according to the germaneness of the amendment after the general debate time is exhausted.

The rule placed on a bill can have an extremely important impact on the bill's chance of passage. Depending on its view of a bill, the Rules Committee can create a rule that will either promote or doom the bill's chance of survival on the floor. When the party leaders want to pass a bill in the same form in which it was received from committee, they may request a closed rule in order to prevent amendments to the bill. Or perhaps because the bill is complex and not suitable for debate among members without specific knowledge of the subject matter, the leadership wants the committee's version to remain intact. Another reason a bill goes to the floor with a closed rule is that it will prevent members from attempting to kill the bill by weighing it down with unpopular amendments.

The committee chair, ranking minority member, and other committee members appear before the Rules Committee to request the desired rule. Any other members of the House who have views on how the bill should be considered on the floor also may appear. Because the work of the Rules Committee is an internal function of the House, no public witnesses are permitted to participate in the Rules Committee session. After a bill has been granted a rule, the House majority leadership schedules the bill and places it on the appropriate calendar of the House. (See box "Timeline of House Floor Proceedings." The proceedings include the opening procedures such as the Pledge of Allegiance and the one-minute speeches of no more than three hundred words that members are allowed

---

TIMELINE OF HOUSE FLOOR PROCEEDINGS

Opening Procedures

Opening business (Pledge of Allegiance, prayer, receipt of messages from Senate or president)
One-minute speeches
Debate on the rule
Vote on the rule
House resolves into Committee of the Whole.

Floor Debate on the Bill (Under Committee of the Whole)

General Debate:

Speaker (or chair) reiterates the rule that will govern debate.
Clerk reads the bill (or simply the title of the bill).
Speaker (or chair) recognizes the floor managers (majority and minority).
General debate begins.
Majority floor manager provides opening remarks.
Minority floor manager provides opening remarks.
Majority floor manager yields time to a partisan colleague for opening remarks.
A colleague rises and speaks for however long he or she is granted.
If he or she exceeds time allowed, may request additional time.
Floor manager has discretion to grant or refuse such requests for additional time (usually gives additional time unless under severe time constraints).
After an individual from one party has spoken, the floor manager usually allows the other party's floor manager to call on individuals from his or her party.
Minority floor manager yields time to a partisan colleague for opening remarks.
A colleague rises and speaks for however long he or she is granted.
If he or she exceeds time allowed, may request additional time.

Floor manager has discretion to grant or refuse such requests for additional time (usually gives additional time unless under severe time constraints).
Majority and minority floor managers continue alternating back and forth until all members who would like to speak have had their chance.
After all members have had their chance to speak, both majority and minority floor managers yield back the balance of their time to the chair.

Amendment Process Begins (generally follows same procedures as markup):

Speaker recognizes clerk.
Clerk reads first section of the bill, opening it for amendments (if rule allows).
Speaker recognizes majority floor manager to call on any colleagues who wish to propose amendments.
Majority floor manager has first opportunity to allow colleagues to rise to propose amendments.
Member proposing the amendment is generally allowed five minutes to offer his or her amendment and explain its substance and rationale.
Debate on the amendment is allowed, with time again parceled out by the floor managers to colleagues on their side of the aisle.
After debate on amendment, it is called to a vote, or all other amendments are offered following the procedures above and a vote is taken only after all amendments are on the floor.
After the majority party has had opportunity to propose and debate amendments, the minority party is allowed to do so.
Votes are taken.
Committee of the Whole rises.
Vote is conducted on the entire bill, including any amendments that were approved.

---

to give on any subject at the start and end of the legislative day.)

The rule, like any other piece of legislation, must be passed by a majority of the House. Once the rule has won approval, the House resolves itself into the Committee of the Whole House on the State of the Union in order to take up pieces of legislation for consideration. The House meets as the Committee of the Whole to facilitate expeditious action; less stringent parliamentary rules apply and fewer members are needed to constitute a quorum to conduct business. The germaneness rule still applies, however, which means that any amendments to the bill must be relevant to the existing legislation or be ruled out of order.

When the House meets as the Committee of the Whole, the Speaker of the House steps down from the rostrum and hands the gavel to a party colleague, who becomes chair of the Committee of the Whole for debating the bill under consideration. The Speaker thus can participate in the consideration of the bill, occasionally even rising to speak on the measure.

General Floor Procedures

The general floor debate on a bill usually proceeds methodically section by section, beginning to end, much as the markup procedures unfolded in committee. The rule adopted by the House for the bill governs the length of the debate, which normally lasts about one or two hours, and "floor managers," usually the committee chair or subcommittee chair and the ranking minority member, control the allocation of the debate time, which is evenly divided between the majority and minority parties. In allocating debate time, the floor managers usually give members of the committee and subcommittee first preference.

The majority floor manager, in opening remarks, introduces the bill. Opening remarks by the minority floor manager follow. The majority floor manager then begins the debate by saying, "Mr. Chairman (or Madam Chairman), I yield myself such time as I may consume." The chair of the Committee of the Whole (who stands at the rostrum at the front of the chamber) then alternates in recognizing the majority and minority floor managers, who in turn yield time, usually two to three minutes, to their partisan colleagues. Some members of Congress rise to praise the bill in its entirety, to praise certain sections of the bill while advocating modifications to other sections, or to offer criticism. Because members can speak only when recognized by their party's floor manager, those wishing to speak usually meet with their party's floor manager prior to the beginning of general debate to work out these logistics ahead of time. During the debate, many members will ask unanimous consent to "revise and extend" their remarks. This action automatically places their written remarks (in addition to their oral ones) in the *Congressional Record*.

Debate expires at the end of the time allotted under the rule, or earlier if all requests for time have been honored. To bring the debate to an end, both floor managers say, "Mr. Chairman (or Madam Chairman), I have no further requests for time and yield back the balance of my time."

Amending and Voting Procedures

At the conclusion of the general debate period, the amending process commences with the second reading of the bill, which is usually done sequentially, either paragraph by paragraph, section by section, or title by title. After the clerk has read section 101, for example, that section is open to amendment. At this point, any member may propose an amendment. The present general House rule requires that members notify their colleagues beforehand of any proposed amendments; the rule may be suspended but usually is not. Amendments also must be submitted to the reading clerk before they are offered.

Amendments are debated under the five-minute rule, which simply specifies that the author of an amendment can speak in support of the amendment for five minutes. Any other member may then speak against the amendment. Customarily, only a few proponents and opponents speak on any given amendment in order to avoid delays in the legislative process.

Members must present germane amendments or they may be subject to a point of order in which the amendment is ruled out of order by the chair of the Committee of the Whole. Once members have debated the merits of an amendment or any amendments of the amendment (these are called second-degree amendments), they vote on the amendment. Votes may be held in several ways, depending on the desires of a sponsor or group of sponsors of any amendment:

- Voice vote
- Vote by raised hands
- Vote by division—ayes and nays standing separately and counted
- Vote by tellers—ayes and nays file down the aisles of the House chamber, depositing red (nay) or green (aye) cards in each ballot box. Each card is signed by the member and recorded in the day's *Congressional Record*.
- Electronic voting—members are given time to insert a voting card into a voting machine to be recorded.

After all debate and voting on amendments are concluded, the Committee of the Whole automatically resolves itself back into the House of Representatives. The Speaker resumes the chair, the chair of the Committee of the Whole House on the State of the Union faces the Speaker from the lower rostrum, bows low, and says, "Mr. Speaker, I wish to report to you the status of H.R. _____," at which point the amended bill is figuratively handed to the Speaker. The Speaker recognizes a member of the group opposing the legislation to offer the recommittal motion, which is one last opportunity for opponents of the bill either to record a vote on their policy alternative or to send the bill back to committee, thus effectively killing the bill. Recommittal motions may take one of two forms, a "straight" recommittal motion or a recommittal with instructions. A straight motion ("I move to recommit the bill to the Committee on _____"), if adopted, kills the bill. The "with instructions" form ("I move to recommit the bill to the Committee on _____ with instructions that it report back forthwith a new bill") gives the opposition to a bill one last chance to pass its own version of the legislation. The recommittal motions are subject to a vote, so if a majority of the chamber does not agree to recommit the bill, the motion fails. After any recommittal motions are entertained, the entire House votes on the legislation. A majority vote is required for approval.

Once a bill has been passed by both the House and the Senate, the versions of the bill approved by each chamber must be reconciled in a conference committee. In conference, the managers for each house, typically members of the bill's subcommittee that originally dealt with the bill and other experts on the bill, meet together to unify the House and Senate versions and agree on any changes that will be made. If these two groups cannot reach an agreement, the bill dies in conference, because the differences must be resolved and ratified by each house before being sent to the president. When the two chambers cannot reconcile their differences, the managers return to their chambers to ask for advice on how to proceed. They then return to the conference and try again. Once the two versions are made into one, each chamber ratifies the final changes and the bill is sent to the president to be signed into law.

This chapter has provided you with a basic overview of the legislative process. Now Chapter 2 will take you through the simulation process itself, reviewing the roles to be played during the committee and floor deliberations and describing the choices of legislation to be debated.

Notes

1. "California; Twenty-Seventh District," *Almanac of American Politics* (New York: Dutton, 2000), 246.

2. Peter Wallsten, "Rogan's Run: The GOP Fights for a Crucial Swing District," *CQ Weekly*, June 10, 2000, 1366.

3. Bill Ainsworth, "California GOP Paid High Price for Unpopular Impeachment," *San Diego Union-Tribune*, January 1, 2001, A3.

4. Wallsten, "Rogan's Run," 1366.

5. Ainsworth, "California GOP." Also see Gregory L. Giroux, "House: GOP Maintains Thin Edge," *CQ Weekly*, November 11, 2000, 2652.

6. Throughout U.S. history, all Speakers of the House have been men. Thus we use the word *he* to refer to those who have already served in the office, not to suggest that only men can hold the position.

7. Roger H. Davidson and Walter J. Oleszek, *Congress and Its Members*, 7th ed. (Washington, D.C.: CQ Press, 2000).

8. Rule XI, House Rules. For other rules pertaining to hearing procedures, see U.S. House of Representatives, Committee on Rules, "House Rules Which Govern the Committee Hearing Process," online at www.house.gov/rules.

9. For further information about House committee hearings, see Richard C. Sachs, *Hearings in the House of Representatives: A Guide for Preparation and Procedure* (Washington, D.C.: Congressional Research Service, 2000). Online at HYPERLINK www.house.gov/rules/RL30539.pdf.

10. 107th Congress Committee Rules, 3(d)(2).

11. Sachs, *Hearings in the House of Representatives*, 21.

12. Stanley Bach, *The Committee Markup Process in the House of Representatives* (Washington, D.C.: Congressional Research Service, 1999). Online at www.house.gov/rules.

13. Stanley Bach, *Points of Order, Rulings, and Appeals in the House of Representatives* (Washington, D.C.: Congressional Research Service, 1998). Online at www.house.gov/rules.

14. Walter J. Oleszek, *Congressional Procedures and the Policy Process*, 5th ed. (Washington, D.C.: CQ Press, 2001), 113.

15. The enacting clause states, "Be it enacted by the Senate and the House of Representatives of the United States of America in Congress assembled." It comes before the actual text of the bill, preceding the table of contents.

CHAPTER 2

Guide to the Simulation

The process by which a bill becomes a law is complex and slow, requiring compromise at every step of the way. In fact, a bill is far more likely to fail than to succeed, because the legislative system favors the opponents of legislation by giving them many opportunities to throw up roadblocks. Many books have been written about Congress as an institution, but it is hard to understand the institution without experiencing it firsthand. This simulation gives participants an opportunity to augment their "textbook" knowledge of Congress with a more personal understanding of congressional politics that can be gained from following a bill after it has been assigned to a committee or committees. This chapter contains an overview of the various responsibilities of a participant in the simulation as well as a brief introduction to the real-life congressional procedures used during committee hearings, committee markup, and floor action.

How the Simulation Works

Each participant in the simulation will play the role of a member of the House of Representatives who participates in lawmaking through committee work (committee hearings and committee markup) and action on the House floor. In their roles as members of Congress, participants will begin to understand the different pressures that are placed on members when crafting and voting on legislation. Many participants also will have an opportunity to play an additional role—that of an interest group spokesperson, committee chair or ranking minority member, Speaker of the House, House clerk, or committee staff person. By playing more than one role, participants will understand the legislative process from at least two different perspectives. In addition, those playing the role

of the interest group spokesperson will understand the importance of interest groups in the legislative process and their influence (or sometimes their lack of influence) over legislation.

Throughout all phases of the simulation, participants will pretend that at least one of the two pieces of legislation described later in this chapter and contained in Part II is currently winding its way through the House of Representatives. Similar bills may have gone through the House or Senate in past years, and participants are free to look to these other bills for ideas on how to improve the legislation on which they will act. The way in which an actual member of Congress voted on these bills and the position that he or she took in the bill's committee hearings may help participants figure out their member's position on the simulated legislation.

Adherence to absolute reality is not essential so long as participants attempt to do so whenever possible. The purpose of the simulation exercise is not for participants to air their own views but to understand the views of the members they are playing and to understand the bill from those members' perspective. Thus if a participant who is a conservative Republican is assigned to play the role of a liberal Democrat, that participant should argue from the perspective of a liberal Democrat. The information provided on actual procedures followed in the House will help participants to play their roles as realistically as possible.

The Role Play

Congratulations on your election to the 107th Congress of the United States! To play your role as a member of Congress effectively you will need to research three broad topics: first, your member's background, past votes, and leadership positions in the Congress; second, your member's district, including how the legislation under consideration will affect your member's constituents; and, third, the legislation on which you will deliberate and vote.

Researching Your Member of Congress

Like an actor preparing to play a part in a film, you will need to thoroughly familiarize yourself with the member of Congress whose role you will play. Actors preparing for a role often spend weeks, even months, studying their character's personality, quirks, mannerisms, likes, and dislikes so that they can accurately assume that role on the big screen. For example, actor Jim Carrey, while playing Andy Kaufman in *The Man on the Moon,* insisted that members of the cast and crew refer to him either as Andy or Tony while on the set (Tony Clinton was an alter ego of Andy Kaufman). He simply attempted to become Andy Kaufman in all ways possible in order to give as convincing a performance as he could. Although you are not expected to spend months researching your member of Congress, you are expected to know the basics (see boxes, "A Guide to Researching Your Member of Congress" and a "Questionnaire on Your Member of Congress," which will help you get started on gathering the pertinent information). Thorough research of your member's background and philosophy will likely reveal what might make him or her sympathetic or opposed to the legislation under consideration. For example, your member might be a Republican who was a police officer before winning a seat in Congress and so may be especially concerned about guns and gun control. Even though Republicans might be more likely to oppose a ban on assault weapons, this member of Congress, as a former police officer, may support the ban. Without knowing the member's past experience in law enforcement you might wrongly decide to vote against the ban.

Researching Your District

By researching your member's district you will understand the issues that are most important to your member's constituents. House districts across the United States vary tremendously both geographically and demographically. For example, the entire state of Wyoming is one House district, while New York City is made up of some nine House districts (based on the 1990 census). Each House district has a different mix of people, industry, physical features, and local concerns. Some districts are strongly Democratic, some are strongly Republican, and others fall somewhere in between. Likewise, the average

A GUIDE TO RESEARCHING YOUR MEMBER OF CONGRESS

The purpose of this worksheet is to guide your research on your member of Congress. Congressional Web sites and your local library are good places to begin collecting the information you need.

1. Describe your member's congressional district. Where is it? What type of district is it (for example, is it urban or rural)? What industries and businesses are important to it? Is it wealthy or poor? Include any other important information about the district.

2. Describe your member's constituency. Are the constituents conservative, moderate, or liberal? How did they vote in past elections? What issues are important to them? (For example, in Long Island, New York, the issue of gun control became crucial in recent elections because of the murders that took place on the Long Island Railroad.) What is their racial/ethnic makeup?

3. How will your member's constituency be affected by the legislation being argued in front of your committee? For example, suppose you serve on the Judiciary Committee. How many of your constituents are members of the National Rifle Association? You can find this information in a variety of ways; be creative.

4. How will your member's party pressure you to vote on the legislation before your committee? Has the party taken a stand on this issue in the past?

5. Has your member received political contributions from either side of the issue that your committee will consider? List the groups that have supported your member in the past.

6. How has your member voted previously on the issue in front of your committee and on related issues? For example, if you are on the Judiciary Committee, know how your member voted on the Brady bill as well as other bills dealing with guns such as the assault weapons ban. *CQ Weekly* or the *Congressional Quarterly Almanac* will help you find this information. If your member is new to Congress, find out if he or she voted on the same issue while serving in an earlier office.

7. Describe your member. Has he or she faced close elections in the past? Is he or she a safe incumbent? What in your member's personal background might have an influence on your feelings toward the legislation on which you will vote?

8. Keep track of your sources.

QUESTIONNAIRE ON YOUR MEMBER OF CONGRESS

Name of member

_____

District: _____

1. Characteristics of District

Partisan makeup:

_____

_____

_____ percentage of district vote won by Bush in
2000 election

_____ percentage of district vote won by Gore in
2000 election

_____ percentage of district vote won by Clinton
in 1996 election

_____ percentage of district vote won by Dole in
1996 election

Urban/rural mix:

_____

_____

Racial makeup:

_____

_____

_____

Largest employers in district:

_____

_____

_____

Groups in district that donate money to member:

_____

_____

_____

_____

2. Member Characteristics

Committees member sits on:

1. _____

   Subcommittees:

   _____

   _____

2. _____

   Subcommittees:

   _____

   _____

3. _____

   Subcommittees:

   _____

   _____

Leadership positions held by member:

_____

_____

_____

Legislative issues member cares about:

_____

_____

_____

_____

Legislation sponsored by member:

_____

_____

_____

Did member face primary challenge in 2000 election?

_____

If so, percentage of vote received in primary:

_____

Percentage of vote received in 2000 general election:

_____

Percentage of vote received in 1998 general election:

_____

income, occupation, religious background, and racial and ethnic backgrounds of individuals within each district vary significantly. How then will your member's district react to the legislation on which you, playing that member, will be required to cast a vote? Constituents' reactions will become clearer as you delve into the economic foundations and social fabric of your member's district. For example, perhaps your member of Congress is a Republican in a district that is almost evenly split between Republicans and Democrats. The Democratic base of the district consists of a large percentage of union workers and union businesses. Now your member must vote on legislation that deals with workplace injuries and is under pressure from the Republican Party leadership to oppose the bill because any further regulation will harm businesses by costing them money. Yet in the end your member, though Republican, votes in favor of the legislation, bowing to the strong pressure from her Democratic constituents because she knows the importance of unions in her reelection.

Researching the Legislation

In your role as a member of the House of Representatives, you will consider at least one piece of legislation. The two bills are:

- H.R. 1415, the Patient Access to Responsible Care Act of 1997, which seeks to protect patients' rights when they receive medical care from a health maintenance organization (HMO)
- H.R. 1595, the Safe and Sober Streets Act of 1999, which seeks to establish a national standard to prohibit the operation of motor vehicles by individuals under the influence of alcohol.

Both bills appear in Part II of this book. In the simulation, you will research at least one of these bills and debate its merits in committee hearings and markup sessions (a membership list of the committees of the 107th Congress, 2001–2002, that would have jurisdiction over such legislation appears in Part II; for the actual testimony of the witnesses who testified for each bill at committee hearings when this legislation was actually introduced, see the instructor's manual on the Web at http://library.cqpress.com/gia).

As an elected representative, you will need to understand all aspects of your committee's legislation—the issues surrounding it and what is in it—so you can make an informed vote and explain your vote to your con-

stituents. Selected background materials on each bill also appear in Part II. These materials detail the history of the issue addressed in the legislation, related laws that may influence the debate, and the ways in which the legislation could affect selected constituencies. Ultimately, will the legislation help or harm your constituents?

The Three Simulation Phases: Committee Hearing, Committee Markup, and Floor Debate

In this simulation, your class or group will enact three phases of the legislative process: the committee hearing in which members of the Congress are able to learn about a piece of legislation directly from those with expertise on the bill's subject matter; the committee markup in which the committee changes and amends the bill in preparation for its presentation to the full House; and the floor debate in which the bill, after being reported out of committee, is debated by the entire membership; perhaps amended; and finally brought up for a vote.

In the first two phases, your class or group, depending on its size, will act as one or more congressional committees. Although legislation in the House typically is referred from a committee to a subcommittee, which then holds the hearings and markup, the simulation will conduct these procedures only at the full committee level to simplify the exercise. Your class or group will conduct committee hearings, committee markup, and run the floor debate for at least one piece of legislation (these activities are discussed in more detail later in this section). The committee hearing is your first opportunity to play your role as a member of Congress. As a member of the committee you are an expert on both the content of the legislation and the ways in which the legislation will affect the people and industries of your district.

During the committee hearing (but not during the committee markup or the floor debate), some participants will also play the role of an interest group representative or other expert who is testifying before the committee. These witnesses will present oral testimony for or against the legislation and answer questions from committee members.

Committee Hearing

As noted, the first phase of the legislative simulation is the committee hearing where members of Congress and the public learn about proposed legislation directly from those with expertise on its subject matter. The committee, led by the chair, calls witnesses to testify and asks witnesses to answer questions and provide clarification where necessary. Because each legislator on the committee is allotted time to question witnesses, legislators will have to draft questions for the witnesses beforehand.

The witnesses who appear before the committee should submit their testimony to the committee ahead of time so that committee members can familiarize themselves with the arguments and perspectives of the witness in preparing their questions (see http://library.cqpress.com/gia for copies of actual witness testimony on the two bills). As a legislator who sits on the committee, whether as committee chair, as the ranking minority member, or as a rank and file member, you are required to ask thoughtful questions of the witnesses about their testimony, such as how the bill can be expected to affect your constituents, or what other ramifications the bill might have for the population or segments of the population.

On each committee the most senior member of the majority party is typically, though not always, the committee chair, and the most senior member of the minor-ity party is the ranking member. The committee chair presides over the hearings. This member sets the tone of the committee hearing by making an opening statement about the legislation being considered and the goals of the hearing. The chair also sets the tone in the way in which he or she treats the witnesses in front of the committee (the specific responsibilities of the committee members, committee chair, ranking member, and interest group witnesses are outlined in the box "Summary of Committee Hearing Responsibilities").

After making opening remarks, the chair calls on the witnesses to testify, one by one. After the witnesses have testified, the committee chair begins the questioning, followed by the ranking minority member. The committee chair determines the time allotted for the questioning of each witness and controls the question period itself by calling on fellow committee members and then enforcing the time limits on questions. The questioning alternates back and forth between Republicans and Democrats until the least senior member on each side of the aisle has been heard. Some committees use a "first come, first heard"

SUMMARY OF COMMITTEE HEARING RESPONSIBILITIES

Member of Congress
• Read witnesses' testimonies prior to the hearing (see http://library.cqpress.com/gia).
• Prepare questions to ask the witnesses.
• Read and understand each section of the legislation under consideration.

Committee chair (the following roles in addition to all of the responsibilities of a member)
• Make an opening statement about the legislation under consideration.
• Decide the order in which witnesses will testify.
• Call on each witness to testify.
• Keep track of the time.
• Recognize colleagues who wish to speak or ask questions of witnesses.
• Allocate time among your party's members.
• Thank each witness for testifying.
• Bring the hearing to a close.

Ranking member (the following roles in addition to all of the responsibilities of a member)
• Make an opening statement about the legislation under consideration.
• Allocate time among your party's members.
• Work with the committee chair.
• Organize your party's members to ensure the outcome you desire.

Interest group witness
• Present testimony.
• Answer members' questions.
• Clarify testimony at member's request.

system in which members are recognized for questions in the order in which they arrived at the session. The chair is the sole judge of the time expended by each member and cannot be questioned officially as to whether the count is accurate. After time expires, the chair usually brings the questioning to an end.

The ranking member of the minority party has organizational duties similar to those of the chair: deciding who in the minority party will be recognized to speak and for how long and, typically, making an opening statement at the hearings. The ranking member's influence in the hearings will depend on that member's relationship with the chair.

If you are one of those playing the role of a witness appearing before a congressional committee, you will have to prepare testimony that explains your group's position on the legislation being considered by the committee. But before writing the testimony, you will first need to learn about the group you are representing. For example, suppose Congress was considering a bill that would legalize the medicinal use of marijuana and the American Medical Association (AMA) was called to testify in favor of the bill. Anyone assigned to play the role of representative of this group would, first, want to learn more about the goals and purpose of the organization by contacting the organization itself, visiting its Web site, and conducting a search of print media such as newspapers and magazines. Second, you will want to learn how your group stands on the legislation. Often, in searching for information on the group you represent, you will uncover statements telling you its exact position on the issue that your committee is considering. The examples of witness testimony for each bill included in Part II can be used as a guide for writing your own testimony (also see the box "Interest Group Worksheet," which will help you get started on your testimony).

If, after all your research, you feel you do not know the subject matter well enough to testify before the committee, do not worry. Some interest groups employ experts whose sole job it is to testify before Congress on legislation within their areas of expertise, but you will not be held to the same expectations. Given the limited time allocated for the role play, the most important task of each witness is to absorb the background information provided in Part II. Once you understand the basic information, you can flesh out your role—either by drawing on life experiences, doing further reading on the subject, or consulting with other participants.

INTEREST GROUP WORKSHEET

The purpose of this worksheet is to get you started on your testimony. After you answer these questions you should have much of the necessary background information on the organization for whom you will be testifying.

1. Describe the group you represent. If a group, what is its membership size? What issues is it concerned with? Where is its headquarters? Is it for profit or nonprofit? Include relevant background information on the individual or group that the committee might be concerned about.

2. What is your group's position on the issue on which you are testifying? Briefly explain.

3. Has your group had success in the past on this or similar issues?

4. You know the members to whom you will be testifying, and you know that getting a bill through committee is extremely important. Do you believe you will be facing a hostile or friendly panel? Has your group made contributions to any of these members in the past? How does your group rate them if the group has a rating system? Do your homework on the members of the committee.

5. What sources are you using to find out about your group?

Committee Markup

After the committee holds hearings, it amends the bill in a committee meeting known as a markup session. The goal of the markup session is to have the committee vote out a final bill for consideration on the floor of the House of Representatives. If the committee approves the legislation and sends it to the House floor, it is said to have "reported favorably on the bill."

During the markup stage, committees engage in detailed deliberations on the legislation (see box "Summary of Committee Markup Responsibilities"). Insights gained from the testimony presented at the hearing may spur committee members to change legislation by striking objectionable sections from the bill, strengthening parts that seem too weak, or otherwise modifying the bill to make it more to their and their constituents' liking. To these ends, members may remove whole sections, add amendments, or rewrite the bill entirely. Changes made to the bill need to be "germane" (or relevant) to the subject matter of the bill. If not germane, the amendment could be ruled out of order by the committee chair. For the simulation, all participants playing the role of a member of Congress are responsible for making suggestions about how the legislation should be altered.

SUMMARY OF COMMITTEE MARKUP RESPONSIBILITIES

Member of Congress
- Prepare opening statements, if any.
- Prepare amendments or changes to the bill.
- Prepare explanations/rationale as to why the committee should incorporate your changes to the legislation.

Committee chair (the following roles in addition to all of the responsibilities of a member)
- Prepare introductory statements about the bill and how the markup will proceed.
- Run the markup session by going through the bill section by section (or by calling on the clerk to read the sections as necessary).
- Recognize colleagues who wish to speak or offer modifications to the bill.
- Mediate disputes between members.
- Make sure amendments are germane to the bill.
- Call for a vote on each suggested modification.
- Call for a final vote when markup is finished.
- Bring markup to a close.

Ranking member (the following roles in addition to all of the responsibilities of a member)
- Assist committee chair in mediating disputes.
- Lead members of minority party in pressing for changes, if appropriate.

Clerk
- Read aloud the bill title and sections as necessary.
- Read aloud each proposed amendment as it is offered.
- Edit bills following markup, incorporating any changes passed in committee.

Committee Staff
- Keep minutes of markup session.
- Prepare report after markup session, summarizing committee action on bill.
- Distribute committee report to the clerk and other members of Congress prior to floor debate.

In general, the same rules utilized by the House during floor procedures apply to committee markup sessions. The chair of the committee usually begins the markup by offering opening remarks and explaining how the committee will proceed throughout the markup. Other members also have an opportunity to make opening statements at this point if they wish. After the opening statements, the committee clerk normally begins to read the bill section by section. Once read, a section is open for discussion and amendment. The bill is usually marked up in order of its titles starting with the first section and moving through until each section has been discussed. The committee chair calls on members, typically by seniority, to suggest changes in the legislation. These changes must be submitted in writing and are read in their entirety before the rest of the committee begins debate on their merits. After the modifications are read aloud, committee members may voice their objections, suggest other modifications, or simply agree to go along with the changes. When the discussion has ceased, the committee votes on the suggested modification to the bill. If a majority of members agree to the changes, the bill is rewritten to reflect those changes. The chair then directs the clerk to read the next section of the bill, and the debate and modification process is repeated. When committee members have already read the bill, they often dispense with its reading by a vote of unanimous consent. After all sections of the bill have been debated and all amendments entertained, the committee then votes on whether to report the bill to the House floor. Again, a majority of yea votes is necessary to dislodge the bill from committee and send it to the full House.

Like in the committee hearing, the committee chair and the ranking member influence the direction of the markup session. If the two members have an amicable relationship, the markup is more likely to work in a bipartisan fashion. If their relationship is contentious, the markup will most likely result in partisan division and the bill will have little chance of long-term survival.

Floor Debate

After the bill is reported out of committee, it must be granted a rule from the House Rules Committee before it can be debated on the floor of the House. The rule specifies how debate will proceed when the legislation reaches the House floor. Because the rule that governs floor debate is like any other piece of legislation, it too must be passed by a majority vote of the House. In this simulation, the Speaker of the House or the simulation leader will decide on the rule for debate and will communicate this rule to the rest of the group. Normally, the entire House would have the option of voting for or against the proposed rule, but to simplify floor procedures in the simulation, this step may be omitted.

Before beginning to debate the merits of a particular piece of legislation, the House goes through several preliminary procedures each morning—among them, one-minute speeches, the Pledge of Allegiance, a prayer, approval of the *Journal* from the previous day's legislative session, and receipt of messages from the Senate or the president. Depending on the amount of time your class or group has set aside for floor debate and the simulation

leader's preferences, these procedures may be omitted without sacrificing the true spirit of the floor debate.

To begin the floor debate on a bill, all legislators gather on the House floor (see box "General Decorum: Some Tips on Being a Representative"). The chamber is divided along partisan lines, with Republicans sitting on the right side of the center aisle that divides the chamber and Democrats aligned on the left (as they face the front of the chamber). The bill's "floor managers," usually the committee chair and ranking minority member from the committee that held hearings and markup, will explain the changes made to the bill in committee and will guide their colleagues through the floor debate (see box "Summary of Floor Debate Responsibilities"). Each floor manager is allotted half of the total time allowed for floor debate and is responsible for calling on colleagues to speak about the bill while the floor debate unfolds. In addition, each floor manager is responsible for meeting with his or her colleagues ahead of time to strategize about how best to use their time on the floor.

During the floor debate, members make changes to (or amend) the bill to either improve or defeat it. Some members of the committee that held hearings and markup will try to convince their colleagues of the bill's worth; others will urge defeat of the bill. The floor debate is usually divided into two separate stages: the general debate and the amendment process. The rule from the Rules Committee usually specifies how much time will be allotted for each phase. In the simulation, about half of the time could

---

GENERAL DECORUM: SOME TIPS ON BEING A REPRESENTATIVE

It is . . . the duty of the House to require its Members in speech or debate to preserve that proper restraint which will permit the House to conduct its business in an orderly manner and without unnecessarily and unduly exciting animosity among its Members or antagonism from those other branches of the Government with which the House is correlated. (*Cannon's Precedents*, 1909)

Here are some tips for conducting yourself properly in House proceedings. For further information on decorum among members, see the Congressional Research Service publication *Decorum in House Debate*, online at www.house.gov/rules/98-572.pdf.

- Always speak to the chair.
- Attract the chair's attention by saying, "Mr. Chairman" (or "Madam Chairman").
- Do not refer to your colleagues directly. For example, if you wish to comment on the remarks of a colleague you would say, "Mr. (or Madam) Chairman, my distinguished colleague from Maryland has just said black is white and I would like to point out that . . ."
- To ask a question or to make a comment while another member is speaking, say, "Mr. (or Madam Chairman), will the gentleman (gentlewoman) yield?"
- Refer to yourself as "I."
- To signify the conclusion of your remarks, say, "I yield back the balance of my time."
- To do something not permitted by the rules, say, "I ask unanimous consent that . . ."
- To enforce a rule, say, "I make a point of order against _____ on the grounds that . . ."

SUMMARY OF FLOOR DEBATE RESPONSIBILITIES

Member of Congress
- Prepare one-minute speech for opening procedures, if appropriate.
- Prepare opening remarks in favor of or opposed to legislation for beginning of general debate.
- Prepare specific amendments for changing the bill.
- Prepare explanations/rationale as to why the House should incorporate your changes to the legislation.

Floor managers (the following roles in addition to all of the responsibilities of a member)
- Convince other House members to support your legislation (lobbying outside of the simulation is encouraged).
- Provide opening remarks to explain the legislation to your colleagues in the chamber.
- Recognize colleagues from your own party and allow them time to speak on the floor.
- Explain the committee's prior actions on the legislation.
- Interact with Speaker or chair of the Committee of the Whole to keep process moving forward smoothly.

Speaker of the House/Chair of the Committee of the Whole
- With the help of the simulation leader, craft the rule from the Rules Committee.
- Preside over the floor debate.
- Call on House clerk to read each section of the bill as necessary.
- Keep track of time, making sure each party receives one-half of the allotted time for the floor debate.
- Rule on germaneness, points of order, etc.
- Call for votes on amendments.
- Call for a final vote on the entire legislation.

Clerk
- Read aloud the bill title and sections as necessary.
- Execute roll call when necessary (that is, call on members by name and record their votes).
- Organize amendments to be offered on the floor (in consultation with floor managers).

be allotted to the general debate and the remaining half to entertaining amendments to the bill.

During the floor debate, you will attempt to convince your fellow members to vote for or against the legislation. The members who are not on your committee know little about the piece of legislation on which they are voting. Supporters of the bill must be able to convince their colleagues of the legislation's merit and the ways that it will influence their constituents. Opponents of the legislation will point out its defects and ways in which it could harm constituents. These arguments can be made in several ways. First, you could request time for a one-minute speech at the start of the legislative proceedings (this request should be made in advance to the Speaker of the House or whoever will preside over floor proceedings). Second, during the general debate you could make an opening statement in favor or opposition to the bill to alert your colleagues to the strengths or weaknesses of the bill. Third, during the amendment phase you could offer an amendment to the bill and take advantage of the five-minute rule that governs amendment procedures. Gener-

ally, members who offer amendments to a piece of legislation on the House floor are allotted five minutes in which to present the substance of the amendment, explaining to their colleagues why they deem the amendment necessary. All three of these speaking opportunities allow you to communicate your thoughts and preferences about the bill to the rest of your colleagues in the House.

Each amendment offered will be subject to a vote. These votes may take place sequentially, immediately after discussion of a particular amendment, or all votes may be postponed until all amendments have been introduced and discussed. Either way, a simple majority is necessary for an amendment to pass and to be added to the original bill. At the end of the floor debate a final recorded vote will be taken on the entire bill. Again, a simple majority is necessary for passage.

Conclusion

Good luck as you embark on your legislative journey. Being a member of Congress is not an easy job and simulating a member is not meant to be easy either. Although you may personally disagree with some of the ideas and votes of your member of Congress, this simulation is supposed to mirror the views of Congress, so try as hard as you can to put forth your member's beliefs, not your own. The most important part of this simulation is to learn and have fun. The better you are at portraying your member, the more fun you and your colleagues will have.

For Further Information

Libraries, the Web, and other sources can provide abundant information about the members of Congress you will play, their districts, the legislation you will deliberate, and the interest groups that will testify. Some information about the legislation has already been collected for you (see Part II), but you will need more and below are some suggestions about where to look. The Web, in particular, will be a very useful resource for participants in this simulation.

Members' Biographies

Barone, Michael, Grant Ujifusa, and Douglas Matthews. *The Almanac of American Politics.* New York: E. P. Dutton, 2000. A guide to members of Congress and their districts. Updated every two years.

Congressional Quarterly. "Campaigns and Elections Magazine" (formerly "CQ's American Voter"). Online at www.campaignline.com. An online magazine that provides information on local, state, and federal political candidates.

Congressional Yellow Book. Washington, D.C.: Washington Monitor. Online at www.leadershipdirectories.com. A guide to congressional staff and committees, with contact information. Updated quarterly.

CQ's Congressional Staff Directory. Washington, D.C.: CQ Press, 2001. A guide to congressional staff and committees, with contact information. Updated quarterly.

CQ's Politics in America 2000: The 106th Congress. Washington, D.C.: Congressional Quarterly, 1999. A guide to members of Congress and their districts.

CQ's Politics in America 2002. Washington, D.C.: Congressional Quarterly, 2001. A guide to members of Congress and their districts.

Roll Call. "Roll Call Congressional Directory." Online at http://capwiz.com/rollcall/home/. Users can locate their member of Congress by zip code and by state.

U.S. Congress. "Biographical Directory of the United States Congress." Online at www.bioguide.congress.gov/biosearch/biosearch.asp. Biographies of members of Continental Congress and Congress, presidents, vice presidents, and Speakers of the House from 1774 to the present.

U.S. Congress. "Congressional Directory." Online at www.access.gpo.gov/congress/cong016.html. An index to members of Congress, committees, staff, and executive branch agencies. Provides biographical information on senators and representatives and includes maps of congressional districts.

U.S. House of Representatives, Office of the Clerk. Online at www.clerkweb.house.gov/. Directories of members of the 104th Congress to the 107th Congress and the biographies of Speakers since the First Congress.

Demographic Profiles of Congressional Districts

U.S. Bureau of the Census. Online at www.census.gov. Domestic economic data, including a variety of statistical data on race, migration, housing, income and poverty, computer use, economic indicators, and labor force. Census data at the national, state, and county levels and for congressional districts online at http://quickfacts.census.gov/qfd/index.html.

Legislative Process

C-SPAN. "Brief Guide to the Legislative Process." Online at congress.nw.dc.us/c-span/process.html. Brief thirteen-step guide to how a bill becomes a law.

———. "Capitol Questions with Ilona Nickels, C-SPAN Resident Congressional Scholar." Online www.cspan.org/questions/.

———. "Congressional Glossary." Online at HYPERLINK http://www.c-span.org/guide/congress/glossary/alphalist.htm.

Marlowe, H. D. "How Congress Works: A Handbook on Congressional Organization and the Legislative Process." Online at www.netlobby.com/hcw.html. Information on the organization and legislative function of Congress, including introduction of a bill, committee action, House floor action, Senate floor action, conference committee action, and presidential approval.

Oleszek, Walter J. *Congressional Procedures and the Policy Process.* 5th ed. Washington, DC: Congressional Quarterly, 2000.

University of Michigan Documents Center. "Legislative Research: A Web-Based Bibliographic Instruction Program." Online at www.lib.umich.edu/libhome/Documents.center/softwarebi/index.html. A comprehensive guide to conducting legislative research.

U.S. House of Representatives. "Congressional Research Service Reports." Online at www.house.gov/rules/crs_reports.htm. Selected full-text reports in the following categories: floor proceedings, special rules, the budget process, relations with the Senate, presidential relations, House committees, introduction and origin of legislative measures, and more.

———. "How Our Laws Are Made." Online at thomas. loc.gov/home/lawsmade.toc.html. Extensive House of Representatives guide to the legislative process with definitions and explanations of each step (summary version is also available).

———. "The Legislative Process—Tying It All Together." Online at www.house.gov/house/Tying_it_all.html. Brief summary of the legislative process in the House.

———. "Rules of the House of Representatives of the United States." Online at www.clerkweb.house.gov/106/docs/rules/contents.htm.

U.S. House of Representatives, Committee on Rules. Online at www.house.gov/rules/.

U.S. House of Representatives, Office of the Clerk. "Historical Highlights." Online at www.clerkweb.house.gov/histrecs/chamber/operat.htm. Overview of the workings of the House.

VOTING RECORDS, BILLS AND LEGISLATION

Congressional Quarterly. *CQ Weekly.* Washington, D.C.: Congressional Quarterly. Available online by subscription. Provides roll call votes, summaries of legislative action, and much more.

Government Printing Office. "GPO Access." Online at www.access.gpo.gov/su_docs/legislative.html. Search congressional bills, calendars, directories, documents, *Congressional Record, Congressional Record Index,* and committee reports. Includes economic indicators, public laws, Privacy Act issuances, a history of bills, *U.S. Government Manual, United States Code,* General Accounting Office (GAO) reports, *Code of Federal Regulations,* and *Federal Register.*

C-SPAN. "Congressional Votes Library." Online at congress.nw.dc.us/cgi-bin/issue.pl?dir=c-span&command=votelib. Votes library searchable by date, member, and subject.

"Project Vote Smart." Online at www.vote-smart.org/. Information on candidates and elected officials. Features congressional voting records and provides links to educational, reference, and political resources.

U.S. House of Representatives. "Roll Call Votes." Online at www.house.gov/.

U.S. House of Representatives, Library of Congress. "THOMAS: Legislative Information on the Internet." Online at thomas.loc.gov/. Indexes bills by subject, sponsor, committee, and stage of legislative process (for example, reported to House), 1973 to the present. Also provides summary of bills and detailed status.

CAMPAIGN FINANCE

Center for Responsive Politics. "Open Secrets.Org." Online at www.opensecrets.org/. Includes extensive database of campaign spending searchable by industry, contributors, and candidates. Also includes information on politicians, special interests, political parties, regulations, and individual donors.

Federal Election Commission (FEC). Summary receipts and disbursements of presidential and congressional candidates. Image files of individual campaign committee reports. Provides financial information on candidates, parties, and political action committees (PACs). Detailed files for individual contributors must be downloaded. Online at http://www.fec.gov/.

"PoliticalMoneyLine." (Owned and operated by Keith Cooper and Tony Raymond.) Online at www.tray.com/fecinfo/. Using data purchased from the Federal Election Commission, site provides information on who gave what and when to specific political candidates and on campaign finance rules and political action committee (PAC) contributions, sorted by type of industry. Data searchable by name, state, political action committee, or individual. Special analyses include contributors by occupation or zip code and candidates receiving the most out-of-state money.

"Project Vote Smart." Online at www.vote-smart.org/. Extensive annotated links to presidential and congressional campaign finance Web sites. Includes lobby group ratings and answers to the National Political Awareness Test.

GENERAL

Newspaper Association of America. "Newspaper Links." Online at www.newspaperlinks.com/. Provides links to hundreds of newspapers from across the country. Newspapers from a member's home state are another good source of information about how that member and his or her district perceive a piece of legislation.

PART II

Legislative Research Materials

H.R. 1415

The following pages contain an abbreviated and condensed version of H.R. 1415, which was considered by the U.S. House of Representatives in 1997. Participants in the simulation will research this bill and debate its merits by holding committee hearings and markup sessions. In the final portion of the simulation, the revised, or marked up, version of this bill will be debated on the House floor. Participants should read the entire bill (as reprinted here) and identify the ways in which it can be changed.

Please note that there are a few important issues that this bill does not discuss that you will be expected to consider. They are:

- Reforming or altering ERISA laws to make HMOs subject to either limited or unlimited lawsuits.
- Internal and External Review Boards as ways for patients to enter into the grievance process.

These issues will be discussed, in part, by some of the witnesses testifying in front of your committee.

105TH CONGRESS
1ST SESSION

H.R. 1415

To amend the Public Health Service Act and the Employee Retirement Income Security Act of 1974 to establish standards for relationships between group health plans and health insurance issuers with enrollees, health professionals, and providers.

IN THE HOUSE OF REPRESENTATIVES

APRIL 23, 1997

Mr. NORWOOD (for himself, Mr. BACHUS, Mr. BAKER, Mr. BARCIA, Mr. BARR of Georgia, Mr. BARRETT of Wisconsin, Mr. BISHOP, Mr. BROWN of Ohio, Mr. CANADY of Florida, Mr. CHAMBLISS, Mr. COBLE, Mr. COBURN, Mr. COMBEST, Mr. COOKSEY, Mr. CRAMER, Mr. DAVIS of Illinois, Mr. DAVIS of Virginia, Mr. DEAL of Georgia, Mr. DEFAZIO, Mr. DICKEY, Mr. DUNCAN, Mr. FILNER, Mr. FOLEY, Mr. FOX of Pennsylvania, Mr. FROST, Mr. GILMAN, Mr. GRAHAM, Mr. HALL of Ohio, Mr. HILLEARY, Mr. HILLIARD, Mr. HINCHEY, Mr. JENKINS, Mrs. KELLY, Mr. KENNEDY of Rhode Island, Mr. KIND, Mr. LAHOOD, Mr. LEWIS of Kentucky, Mr. LINDER, Mr. LIVINGSTON, Mrs. MALONEY of New York, Mr. MCHALE, Mr. MCHUGH, Mrs. MORELLA, Mrs. MYRICK, Mr. NETHERCUTT, Mr. PALLONE, Mr. PICKERING, Mr. RANGEL, Mr. RIGGS, Mrs. ROUKEMA, Mr. SANDERS, Mr. SCARBOROUGH, Mr. SENSENBRENNER, Mr. SHADEGG, Mr. SOLOMON, Mr. SPENCE, Mr. STRICKLAND, Mr. TOWNS, Mr. WALSH, Mr. WICKER, Mr. WISE, Ms. WOOLSEY, Mr. WEYGAND, Mr. CHRISTENSEN, Mr. COLLINS, and Mr. WAMP) introduced the following bill; which was referred to the Committee on Commerce, and in addition to the Committee on Education and the Workforce, for a period to be subsequently determined by the Speaker, in each case for consideration of such provisions as fall within the jurisdiction of the committee concerned

---

A BILL

To amend the Public Health Service Act and the Employee Retirement Income Security Act of 1974 to establish standards for relationships between group health plans and health insurance issuers with enrollees, health professionals, and providers.

1   *Be it enacted by the Senate and House of Representatives of the*

2   *United States of America in Congress assembled,*

3   **SECTION 1. SHORT TITLE; TABLE OF CONTENTS.**

4   (a) SHORT TITLE—This Act may be cited as the 'Patient Access

5   to Responsible Care Act of 1997'.

6   (b) TABLE OF CONTENTS—The table of contents of this Act is

7   as follows:

2

1   'Sec. 1. Short title; table of contents.

2   'Sec. 2. Patient protection standards under the Public Health

3 Service Act.

4 **Part C—Patient Protection Standards**

5   'Sec. 2770. Notice; additional definitions; construction.

6   'Sec. 2771. Enrollee access to care.

7   'Sec. 2772. Enrollee choice of health professionals and providers.

8   'Sec. 2773. Nondiscrimination against enrollees and in the selec-

9 tion of health professionals; equitable access to networks.

10   'Sec. 2774. Prohibition of interference with certain medical com-

11 munications.

12   'Sec. 2775. Development of plan policies.

13   'Sec. 2776. Due process for enrollees.

14   'Sec. 2777. Due process for health professionals and providers.

15   'Sec. 2778. Information reporting and disclosure.

16   'Sec. 2779. Confidentiality; adequate reserves.

17   'Sec. 2780. Quality improvement program.

18   'Sec. 3. Patient protection standards under the Employee Retire-

19 ment Income Security Act of 1974.

20   'Sec. 4. Non-preemption of State law respecting liability of group

21 health plans.

22 **SEC. 2. PATIENT PROTECTION STANDARDS UNDER THE**

23 **PUBLIC HEALTH SERVICE ACT.**

24   (a) Patient Protection Standards—Title XXVII of the Public

25 Health Service Act is amended—

26   (1) by redesignating part C as part D, and

27   (2) by inserting after part B the following new part:

28 **'Part C—Patient Protection Standards**

29 **'SEC. 2770. NOTICE; ADDITIONAL DEFINITIONS; CON-**

30 **STRUCTION.**

31   '(a) NOTICE—A health insurance issuer under this part shall

32 comply with the notice requirement under section 711(d) of the

33 Employee Retirement Income Security Act of 1974 with respect to the

3

1 requirements of this part as if such section applied to such issuer and

2 such issuer were a group health plan.

3   '(b) ADDITIONAL DEFINITIONS—For purposes of this part:

4   '(1) ENROLLEE—The term 'enrollee' means, with respect to

5 health insurance coverage offered by a health insurance issuer, an

6 individual enrolled with the issuer to receive such coverage.

7   '(2) HEALTH PROFESSIONAL—The term 'health profes-

8 sional' means a physician or other health care practitioner licensed,

9 accredited, or certified to perform specified health services consistent

10 with State law.

11   '(3) NETWORK—The term 'network' means, with respect to a

12 health insurance issuer offering health insurance coverage, the par-

13 ticipating health professionals and providers through whom the plan

14 or issuer provides health care items and services to enrollees.

15   '(4) NETWORK COVERAGE—The term 'network coverage'

16 means health insurance coverage offered by a health insurance issuer

17 that provides or arranges for the provision of health care items and

18 services to enrollees through participating health professionals and

19 providers.

20   '(5) PARTICIPATING—The term 'participating' means, with

21 respect to a health professional or provider, a health professional or

22 provider that provides health care items and services to enrollees

23 under network coverage under an agreement with the health insur-

24 ance issuer offering the coverage.

25   '(6) PRIOR AUTHORIZATION—The term 'prior authoriza-

26 tion' means the process of obtaining prior approval from a health in-

27 surance issuer as to the necessity or appropriateness of receiving

28 medical or clinical services for treatment of a medical or clinical

29 condition.

30   '(7) PROVIDER—The term 'provider' means a health organi-

31 zation, health facility, or health agency that is licensed, accredited, or

32 certified to provide health care items and services under applicable

33 State law.

4

1   '(8) SERVICE AREA—The term 'service area' means, with re-

2 spect to a health insurance issuer with respect to health insurance cov-

3 erage, the geographic area served by the issuer with respect to the

4 coverage.

5   '(9) UTILIZATION REVIEW—The term 'utilization review'

6 means prospective, concurrent, or retrospective review of health care

7 items and services for medical necessity, appropriateness, or quality

8 of care that includes prior authorization requirements for coverage of

9 such items and services.

10   '(c) NO REQUIREMENT FOR ANY WILLING PROVIDER—

11 Nothing in this part shall be construed as requiring a health insurance

12 issuer that offers network coverage to include for participation every

13 willing provider or health professional who meets the terms and con-

14 ditions of the plan or issuer.

15 **'SEC. 2771. ENROLLEE ACCESS TO CARE.**

16   '(a) GENERAL ACCESS—

17   '(1) IN GENERAL—Subject to paragraphs (2), and (3), a

18 health insurance issuer shall establish and maintain adequate

19 arrangements, as defined by the applicable State authority, with a

20 sufficient number, mix, and distribution of health professionals and

21 providers to assure that covered items and services are available and

22 accessible to each enrollee under health insurance coverage—

23   '(A) in the service area of the issuer;

24   '(B) in a variety of sites of service;

25   '(C) with reasonable promptness (including reasonable

26 hours of operation and after-hours services);

27   '(D) with reasonable proximity to the residences and work-

28 places of enrollees;   and

29   '(E) in a manner that—

30   '(i) takes into account the diverse needs of enrollees, and

31   '(ii) reasonably assures continuity of care.

32   For a health insurance issuer that serves a rural or medically un-

33 derserved area, the issuer shall be treated as meeting the requirement

5

1 of this subsection if the issuer has arrangements with a sufficient num-

2 ber, mix, and distribution of health professionals and providers having

3 a history of serving such areas. The use of telemedicine and other inno-

4 vative means to provide covered items and services by a health insur-

5 ance issuer that serves a rural or medically underserved area shall also

6 be considered in determining whether the requirement of this subsec-

7 tion is met.

8   '(2) RULE OF CONSTRUCTION—Nothing in this subsection

9 shall be construed as requiring a health insurance issuer to have

10 arrangements that conflict with its responsibilities to establish meas-

11 ures designed to maintain quality and control costs.

12   '(3) DEFINITIONS—For purposes of paragraph (1):

13   '(A) MEDICALLY UNDERSERVED AREA—The term

14 'medically underserved area' means an area that is designated as a

15 health professional shortage area under section 332 of the Public

16 Health Service Act or as a medically underserved area for purposes of

17 section 330 or 1302(7) of such Act.

18   '(B) RURAL AREA—The term 'rural area' means an area

19 that is not within a Standard Metropolitan Statistical Area or a New

20 England County Metropolitan Area (as defined by the Office of Man-

21 agement and Budget).

22 (b) EMERGENCY AND URGENT CARE—

23   (1) IN GENERAL—A health insurance issuer shall—

24   '(A) assure the availability and accessibility of medically or

25 clinically necessary emergency services and urgent care services

26 within the service area of the issuer 24 hours a day, 7 days a week;

27   '(B) require no prior authorization for items and services

28 furnished in a hospital emergency department to an enrollee (without

29 regard to whether the health professional or hospital has a contrac-

30 tual or other arrangement with the issuer) with symptoms that would

31 reasonably suggest to a prudent layperson an emergency medical

32 condition (including items and services described in subparagraph

33 (C)(iii));

6

1   '(C) cover (and make reasonable payments for)—

2   '(i) emergency services,

3   '(ii) services that are not emergency services but are de-

4   scribed in subparagraph (B),

5   '(iii) medical screening examinations and other ancillary

6   services necessary to diagnose, treat, and stabilize an emergency med-

7   ical condition, and

8   '(iv) urgent care services, without regard to whether the

9   health professional or provider furnishing such services has a contrac-

10   tual (or other) arrangement with the issuer; and

11   '(D) make prior authorization determinations for—

12   '(i) services that are furnished in a hospital emergency de-

13   partment (other than services described in clauses (i) and (iii) of sub-

14   paragraph (C)), and

15   '(ii) urgent care services, within the time periods specified

16   in (or pursuant to) section 2776(a)(8).

17   (2) DEFINITIONS—For purposes of this subsection:

18   '(A) EMERGENCY MEDICAL CONDITION—The term

19   'emergency medical condition' means a medical condition (including

20   emergency labor and delivery) manifesting itself by acute symptoms of

21   sufficient severity (including severe pain) such that a prudent lay-

22   person, who possesses an average knowledge of health and medicine,

23   could reasonably expect the absence of immediate medical attention

24   could reasonably be expected to result in—

25   '(i) placing the patient's health in serious jeopardy,

26   '(ii) serious impairment to bodily functions, or

27   '(iii) serious dysfunction of any bodily organ or part.

28   '(B) EMERGENCY SERVICES—The term 'emergency serv-

29   ices' means health care items and services that are necessary for the di-

30   agnosis, treatment, and stabilization of an emergency medical condition.

31   '(C) URGENT CARE SERVICES—The term 'urgent care

32   services' means health care items and services that are necessary for

33   the treatment of a condition that—

7

1   '(i) is not an emergency medical condition,

2   '(ii) requires prompt medical or clinical treatment, and

3   '(iii) poses a danger to the patient if not treated in a

4   timely manner, as defined by the applicable State authority in consul-

5   tation with relevant treating health professionals or providers.

6   '(c) SPECIALIZED SERVICES—

7   '(1) IN GENERAL—A health insurance issuer offering net-

8   work coverage shall demonstrate that enrollees have access to special-

9   ized treatment expertise when such treatment is medically or clini-

10   cally indicated in the professional judgment of the treating health pro-

11   fessional, in consultation with the enrollee.

12   '(2) DEFINITION—For purposes of paragraph (1), the term

13   'specialized treatment expertise' means expertise in diagnosing or

14   treating—

15   '(A) unusual diseases or conditions, or

16   '(B) diseases and conditions that are unusually difficult to

17   diagnose or treat.

18   '(d) INCENTIVE PLANS—

19   '(1) IN GENERAL—In the case of a health insurance issuer

20   that offers network coverage, any health professional or provider in-

21   centive plan operated by the issuer with respect to such coverage shall

22   meet the following requirements:

23   '(A) No specific payment is made directly or indirectly under

24   the plan to a professional or provider or group of professionals or

25   providers as an inducement to reduce or limit medically necessary

26   services provided with respect to a specific enrollee.

27   '(B) If the plan places such a professional, provider, or group

28   at substantial financial risk (as determined by the Secretary) for serv-

29   ices not provided by the professional, provider, or group, the issuer—

30   '(i) provides stop-loss protection for the professional,

31   provider, or group that is adequate and appropriate, based on stan-

32   dards developed by the Secretary that take into account the number of

33   professionals or providers placed at such substantial financial risk in

8

1 the group or under the coverage and the number of individuals en-

2 rolled with the issuer who receive services from the professional,

3 provider, or group, and

4   '(ii) conducts periodic surveys of both individuals enrolled

5 and individuals previously enrolled with the issuer to determine the

6 degree of access of such individuals to services provided by the issuer

7 and satisfaction with the quality of such services.

8   '(C) The issuer provides the Secretary with descriptive in-

9 formation regarding the plan, sufficient to permit the Secretary to de-

10 termine whether the plan is in compliance with the requirements of

11 this paragraph.

12   (2) In this subsection, the term 'health professional or provider

13 incentive plan' means any compensation arrangement between a

14 health insurance issuer and a health professional or provider or pro-

15 fessional or provider group that may directly or indirectly have the

16 effect of reducing or limiting services provided with respect to individ-

17 uals enrolled with the issuer.

18 **'SEC. 2772. ENROLLEE CHOICE OF HEALTH PROFESSION-**

19 **ALS AND PROVIDERS.**

20   '(a) CHOICE OF PERSONAL HEALTH PROFESSIONAL—A

21 health insurance issuer shall permit each enrollee under network cov-

22 erage to—

23   (1) select a personal health professional from among the partic-

24 ipating health professionals of the issuer, and

25   (2) change that selection as appropriate.

26   '(b) POINT-OF-SERVICE OPTION—

27   (1) IN GENERAL—If a health insurance issuer offers to en-

28 rollees health insurance coverage which provides for coverage of serv-

29 ices only if such services are furnished through health professionals

30 and providers who are members of a network of health professionals

31 and providers who have entered into a contract with the issuer to pro-

32 vide such services, the issuer shall also offer to such enrollees (at the

33 time of enrollment) the option of health insurance coverage which pro-

9

1   vides for coverage of such services which are not furnished through

2   health professionals and providers who are members of such a network.

3   (2) FAIR PREMIUMS—The amount of any additional pre-

4   mium required for the option described in paragraph (1) may not ex-

5   ceed an amount that is fair and reasonable, as established by the ap-

6   plicable State authority, in consultation with the National Association

7   of Insurance Commissioners, based on the nature of the additional

8   coverage provided.

9   (3) COST-SHARING—Under the option described in para-

10 graph (1), the health insurance coverage shall provide for reimburse-

11 ment rates for covered services offered by health professionals and

12 providers who are not participating health professionals or providers

13 that are not less than the reimbursement rates for covered services of-

14 fered by participating health professionals and providers. Nothing in

15 this paragraph shall be construed as protecting an enrollee against

16 balance billing by a health professional or provider that is not a par-

17 ticipating health professional or provider.

18   '(c) CONTINUITY OF CARE—A health insurance issuer offering

19 network coverage shall—

20   (1) ensure that any process established by the issuer to coor-

21 dinate care and control costs does not create an undue burden, as de-

22 fined by the applicable State authority, for enrollees with special

23 health care needs or chronic conditions;

24   (2) ensure direct access to relevant specialists for the contin-

25 ued care of such enrollees when medically or clinically indicated in the

26 judgment of the treating health professional, in consultation with the

27 enrollee;

28   (3) in the case of an enrollee with special health care needs or

29 a chronic condition, determine whether, based on the judgment of the

30 treating health professional, in consultation with the enrollee, it is

31 medically or clinically necessary to use a specialist or a care coordina-

32 tor from an interdisciplinary team to ensure continuity of care; and

10

1   (4) in circumstances under which a change of health profes-

2 sional or provider might disrupt the continuity of care for an enrollee,

3 such as—

4   '(A) hospitalization, or

5   '(B) dependency on high-technology home medical equip-

6 ment, provide for continued coverage of items and services furnished

7 by the health professional or provider that was treating the enrollee

8 before such change for a reasonable period of time.

9   For purposes of paragraph (4), a change of health professional or

10 provider may be due to changes in the membership of an issuer's

11 health professional and provider network, changes in the health cov-

12 erage made available by an employer, or other similar circumstances.

13 **'SEC. 2773. NONDISCRIMINATION AGAINST ENROLLEES**

14 **AND IN THE SELECTION OF HEALTH PROFESSIONALS; EQ-**

15 **UITABLE ACCESS TO NETWORKS.**

16   '(a) NONDISCRIMINATION AGAINST ENROLLEES—No

17 health insurance issuer may discriminate (directly or through con-

18 tractual arrangements) in any activity that has the effect of discrimi-

19 nating against an individual on the basis of race, national origin, gen-

20 der, language, socioeconomic status, age, disability, health status, or

21 anticipated need for health services.

22   '(b) NONDISCRIMINATION IN SELECTION OF NETWORK

23 HEALTH PROFESSIONALS—A health insurance issuer offering net-

24 work coverage shall not discriminate in selecting the members of its

25 health professional network (or in establishing the terms and condi-

26 tions for membership in such network) on the basis of—

27   (1) the race, national origin, gender, age, or disability (other

28 than a disability that impairs the ability of an individual to provide

29 health care services or that may threaten the health of enrollees) of

30 the health professional; or

31   (2) the health professional's lack of affiliation with, or ad-

32 mitting privileges at, a hospital (unless such lack of affiliation is a re-

11

1 sult of infractions of quality standards and is not due to a health pro-

2 fessional's type of license).

3   '(c) NONDISCRIMINATION IN ACCESS TO HEALTH

4 PLANS—While nothing in this section shall be construed as an 'any

5 willing provider' requirement (as referred to in section 2770(c)), a

6 health insurance issuer shall not discriminate in participation, reim-

7 bursement, or indemnification against a health professional, who is

8 acting within the scope of the health professional's license or certifica-

9 tion under applicable State law, solely on the basis of such license or

10 certification.

11 **'SEC. 2774. PROHIBITION OF INTERFERENCE WITH CER-**

12 **TAIN MEDICAL COMMUNICATIONS.**

13   '(a) IN GENERAL—The provisions of any contract or agreement,

14 or the operation of any contract or agreement, between a health insur-

15 ance issuer and a health professional shall not prohibit or restrict the

16 health professional from engaging in medical communications with his

17 or her patient.

18   '(b) NULLIFICATION—Any contract provision or agreement de-

19 scribed in subsection (a) shall be null and void.

20   '(c) MEDICAL COMMUNICATION DEFINED—For purposes of

21 this section, the term 'medical communication' means a communica-

22 tion made by a health professional with a patient of the health profes-

23 sional (or the guardian or legal representative of the patient) with re-

24 spect to—

25   (1) the patient's health status, medical care, or legal treatment

26 options;

27   (2) any utilization review requirements that may affect treat-

28 ment options for the patient; or

29   (3) any financial incentives that may affect the treatment of

30 the patient.

31 **'SEC. 2775. DEVELOPMENT OF PLAN POLICIES.**

32   'A health insurance issuer that offers network coverage shall es-

33 tablish mechanisms to consider the recommendations, suggestions,

12

1 and views of enrollees and participating health professionals and

2 providers regarding—

3   (1) the medical policies of the issuer (including policies relat-

4 ing to coverage of new technologies, treatments, and procedures);

5   (2) the utilization review criteria and procedures of the issuer;

6   (3) the quality and credentialing criteria of the issuer; and

7   (4) the medical management procedures of the issuer.

The Committee

Roster

What follows is the roster of the House Energy and Commerce Committee of the 107th Congress (2001–2002). H.R. 1415 was assigned to this committee in 1997, but you will play the role of one of the members of the current committee. Members are listed in order of seniority and are grouped by their respective parties. The most senior member of the majority party is referred to as the committee chair and the most senior member of the minority party is referred to as the ranking member.

House Committee on Energy and Commerce, 107th Congress (2001–2002)

Republicans (in order of seniority)

W. J. (Billy) Tauzin, La.-3 (chairman)
Michael Bilirakis, Fla.-9
Joe Barton, Tex.-6
Fred Upton, Mich.-6
Clifford B. Stearns, Fla.-6
Paul E. Gillmor, Ohio-5
James C. Greenwood, Pa.-8
Christopher Cox, Calif.-47
John Nathan Deal, Ga.-9
Steve Largent, Okla.-1
Richard M. Burr, N.C.-5
Edward Whitfield, Ky.-1
Greg Ganske, Iowa-4
Charles W. Norwood, Ga.-10
Barbara L. Cubin, Wyo.-AL
John Shimkus, Ill.-20
Heather Wilson, N.M.-1
John B. Shadegg, Ariz.-4
Charles W. (Chip) Pickering, Miss.-3
Vito J. Fossella, N.Y.-13
Roy Blunt, Mo.-7
Thomas M. Davis, Va.-11
Edward Bryant, Tenn.-7
Robert L. Ehrlich, Md.-2
Steve Buyer, Ind.-5
George Radanovich, Calif.-19
Joe Pitts, Pa.-16
Mary Bono, Calif.-44
Gregory Walden, Ore.-2
Lee Terry, Neb.-2

Democrats (in order of seniority)

John D. Dingell, Mich.-16 (ranking member)
Henry A. Waxman, Calif.-29
Edward J. Markey, Mass.-7
Ralph M. Hall, Tex.-4
Rick Boucher, Va.-9
Edolphus Towns, N.Y.-10
Frank Pallone, N.J.-6
Sherrod Brown, Ohio-13
Bart Gordon, Tenn.-6
Peter Deutsch, Fla.-20
Bobby L. Rush, Ill.-1
Anna G. Eshoo, Calif.-14
Bart Stupak, Mich.-1
Eliot L. Engel, N.Y.-17
Thomas C. Sawyer, Ohio-14
Albert R. Wynn, Md.-4
Gene Green, Tex.-29
Karen McCarthy, Mo.-5
Ted Strickland, Ohio-6
Diana Degette, Colo.-1
Thomas Mark Barrett, Wisc.-5
William P. Luther, Minn.-6
Lois Capps, Calif.-22

AL = At large.

Witness List

The following witnesses testified for or against H.R. 1415 in the hearings before the House Energy and Commerce Committee. The chair of the committee will choose the order in which they will testify in the simulation. For the text of the testimonies, see http://library.cqpress.com/gia.

Witnesses against the Bill

Karen Ignagni, American Association of Health Plans
Connie Baron, Texas Medical Association
Rob Johnson, Eastman Chemical Company, on behalf of the National Association of Manufacturers

Witnesses for the Bill

Judith Lichtman, Women's Legal Defense Fund
Carol Anderson, Center for Patient Advocacy
Russ Newman, American Psychological Association

Background Materials on H.R. 1415

Participants will find the following background materials on H.R. 1415 useful in familiarizing themselves with the issues dealt with in the bill. These materials detail the history of the issue, related laws that may influence the debate, and the ways in which the legislation could affect elected constituencies.

Patients' Rights

KENNETH JOST

M innesota computer executive Patrick Shea thought he should see a cardiologist. He had been experiencing shortness of breath and dizzy spells. And heart disease ran in his family.

But Shea's physician assured him a specialist wasn't necessary and refused to give him the written referral required by his health plan. Instead, he told Shea that his problems were stress-related and that he was too young to have heart problems.

Later, while on an overseas business trip, Shea suffered chest pains so severe that he was hospitalized and had to return home. But his doctor still dismissed his concerns.

Shea never saw a specialist. He died in March 1993, less than a year later, leaving his wife Dianne with two young children and troubling questions. He was 40. An autopsy disclosed that Shea had suffered from arteriosclerosis — blocked arteries — which might have been corrected with cardiac bypass surgery.

"We repeatedly asked for referral to a cardiologist," Dianne later told a Minnesota legislative committee. "Not only were our pleas ignored, we were assured time and time again that our fears were unfounded."

In the months that followed, Dianne sought to discover how a man who had always followed his doctor's advice could die of an undiagnosed disease. What she found shook her confidence not only in their own doctors but also in the health care that more than 150 million Americans receive today from so-called managed-care systems: health maintenance organizations (HMOs) and similar network health-care plans.[1]

Supporters say managed care helps provide affordable, high-quality health care at a time when patients,

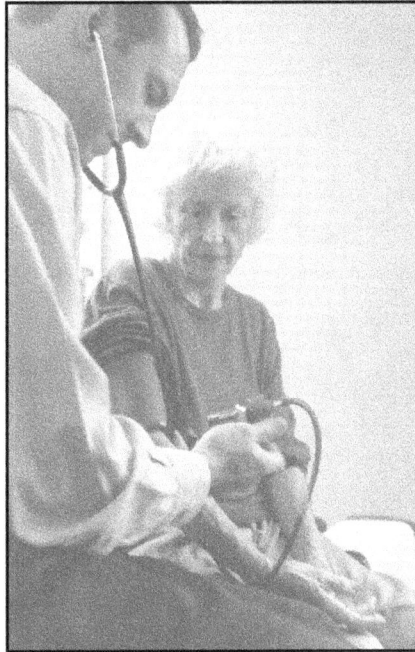

Updated by Adriel Bettelheim, December 1, 2000. Originally published in *The CQ Researcher* February 6, 1998.

health-care providers, insurers and employers are all straining to keep down costs. But Dianne became convinced from the inquiry she and her lawyers made that cost controls helped kill her husband.

She claims in a wrongful death lawsuit that Shea's doctor had an undisclosed financial conflict of interest in refusing to refer him to a cardiologist because he received extra compensation from their HMO, Medica, for not sending patients to specialists.

The defendants in the federal court suit — Shea's doctors, their HMO clinic and Medica — deny that the doctors' compensation in any way depended on rejecting Shea's request to see a specialist. "Sheer speculation," Medica's lawyers say. The defendants also deny they were negligent in failing to diagnose Shea's heart disease. A trial in the case is expected later this year.[2]

Dianne Shea, meanwhile, has begun advocating reform of managed care. She urged the Minnesota Legislature to require health insurers to

disclose their "payment methodology" — information she says that might have prompted Shea to ignore his doctor's advice and see a cardiologist. "People have to understand that health care is a business," she says. "Just as we would never buy an investment blindly, we just cannot trust our doctors blindly."

The state Legislature last year passed a weakened version of Shea's proposal, requiring disclosure of the financial arrangements only on the patient's request. Minnesota thus became one of more than 30 states to pass legislation in the past three years aimed at strengthening the rights of patients enrolled in managed care — by far the dominant form of health care in the United States. *(See chart, p. 46.)*

Congress is also considering legislation that would impose far-reaching regulations on managed-care systems and possibly make it easier to sue health insurers for malpractice. Consumer and patient advocacy groups as well as the American Medical Association (AMA) are generally backing the proposals as part of an envisioned "Patients' Bill of Rights." However, the proposals are strongly opposed by health-care insurers and employers, who so far have thwarted any large-scale reform effort.

The efforts reflect a widespread belief that patients are being harmed in the shift away from traditional "fee-for-service" health insurance, which gave consumers greater freedom in choosing their own doctors and doctors greater freedom in prescribing treatment that insurers would pay for.

"Patients feel less personally taken care of, that they have interactions with too many health-care providers, that there's too much red tape in getting access to the specialists," says Myrl Weinberg, president of the National Health Council, a coalition

Managed-Care Plans Continue to Grow

The number of workers in managed-care health plans outnumbered those in traditional plans by nearly 6-to-1 in 1997, reflecting the continuing shift away from traditional plans in recent years.

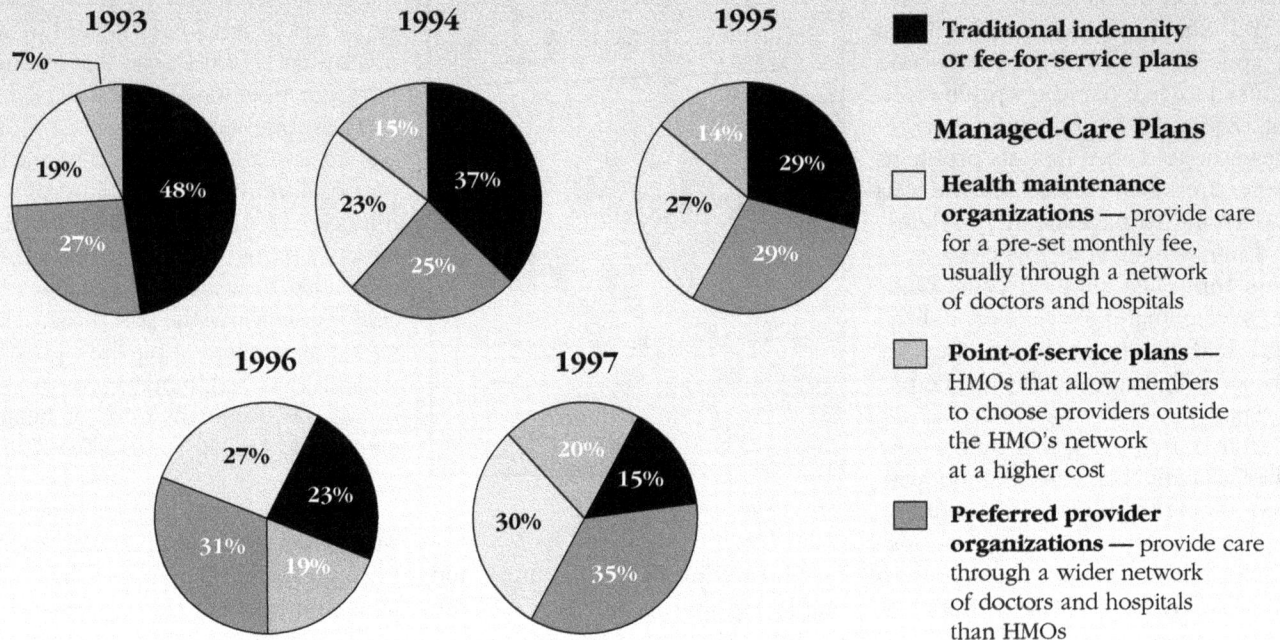

1993

7%
19%
48%
27%

1994

15%
37%
23%
25%

1995

14%
29%
27%
29%

1996

27%
23%
31%
19%

1997

20%
15%
30%
35%

■ **Traditional indemnity or fee-for-service plans**

Managed-Care Plans

□ **Health maintenance organizations** — provide care for a pre-set monthly fee, usually through a network of doctors and hospitals

▨ **Point-of-service plans** — HMOs that allow members to choose providers outside the HMO's network at a higher cost

▨ **Preferred provider organizations** — provide care through a wider network of doctors and hospitals than HMOs

Note: Percentages do not add up to 100 because of rounding. The survey includes all employers with 10 or more employees.

Source: Mercer/Foster Higgins "National Survey of Employer-Sponsored Health Plans," 1997.

of more than 40 patient advocacy groups, such as the American Cancer Society and American Heart Association, as well as major drug manufacturers and health insurers.

But health insurance industry officials insist that patients actually receive better care under managed-care plans.

"There's a tremendous possibility [with HMOs] to receive better, more integrated care," says Karen Ignagni, president of the American Association of Health Plans (AAHP). She says greater coordination among health-care providers also enhances

accountability. "We've put in place the beginnings of quality measurement so that we can ensure significant improvements," she says.

Critics of managed care generally stop short of blaming it for an overall decline in the quality of health care. "For the most part, the studies have shown that the care is relatively the same," says Thomas Reardon, an Oregon physician and chairman of the AMA's Board of Trustees.

But the critics cite cases like Shea's to argue that managed-care plans have an incentive to skimp on care at the patient's expense. "There are

pluses and minuses," says Adrienne Mitchem, legislative counsel for Consumers Union. "Some of the minuses are the overriding cost pressures. With traditional fee-for-service, you had the financial incentives to overtreat. With managed care, you have the financial incentives to undertreat."

Managed-care advocates indeed take credit for helping contain health-care cost increases, which rose at double-digit rates in the late 1980s and early 1990s — and now feel unjustly blamed for the difficulties that patients and providers face in adjusting to the changes.

"The public said to do something about health-care inflation, and we've been largely successful in doing that," says former Rep. Bill Gradison, R-Ohio, president of the Health Insurance Association of America (HIAA), which includes companies offering both managed care and fee-for-service insurance.

"Now, patients are saying, 'Hold on, we don't like the way you're doing it,'" Gradison continues. "The pace of change is bewilderingly fast and off-putting to a lot of people, and I mean not just the patients but the providers as well."

Gradison warns that new regulations "run the risk of increasing the cost of health plans and discouraging innovation." But critics say some changes are needed. "Managed care can do a lot of things well, but it needs to be regulated differently than we're now regulating it," says Lawrence Gostin, a health-law expert at Georgetown University Law Center.

The proposal with the most bipartisan support in Congress is a managed-care bill sponsored in the House by Reps. Charlie Norwood, R-Ga., and John Dingell, D-Mich. Norwood, a dentist, says he wants to "reverse what's going on in this country in health care." But while the measure won the support of 68 Republicans in 1999, Republican leaders have refused to endorse it.

"We've gone from patients having the right to choose their own doctors to patients being denied care and being denied the right to choose their own doctors to save money," Norwood says. "I don't oppose managed care, but I think there needs to be rules and regulations."

President Clinton also strongly endorsed managed-care reform. "Medical decisions ought to be made by medical doctors, not insurance company accountants," Clinton said in his 1998 State of the Union address. The line drew bipartisan applause from lawmakers that continued as Clinton spelled out his proposal:

"I urge this Congress to reach across the aisle and write into law a consumer bill of rights that says this: 'You have the right to know all your medical options, not just the cheapest. You have the right to choose the doctor you want for the care you need. You have the right to emergency room care, wherever and whenever you need it. You have the right to keep your medical records confidential.' Now, traditional care or managed care, every American deserves quality care."

Clinton's plea covered the main parts of a "Patients' Bill of Rights" issued by a 34-member commission he created in 1997. But he made no specific reference to one of its most contentious recommendations: a proposal to give patients greater ability to contest decisions by health plans to deny coverage for medical treatment.

Earlier, the administration also proposed separate legislation aimed at protecting patients' medical information. The privacy issue has become increasingly worrisome as computers have become more capable of accessing the most personal information. But the administration's proposals were widely criticized as too weak — in particular for giving law enforcement agencies broad discretion to obtain medical records without a patient's consent (see p. 48).

When Congress and state legislatures continue to ponder managed-care reform, these are some of the questions likely to be considered:

Should managed-care health plans be required to make it easier for patients to see specialists outside the plan's network of physicians?

The most visible difference between managed-care health plans and traditional fee-for-service insurance involves choosing a doctor and deciding when to seek treatment. Traditional insurance plans leave those choices to the patient; managed-care plans limit the patient's options.

Typically, a patient who enrolls in an HMO, like Patrick Shea, selects a "primary-care provider" from its network of doctors. That doctor then functions as a "gatekeeper" — overseeing the patient's health care and deciding when the patient needs to be referred to a specialist. [3]

The earliest group-health plans, in the 1920s and '30s, centralized medical decisions both to improve health care and lower costs. But since the federal government began promoting HMOs in the '70s, and later as for-profit managed-care plans came to dominate the industry, the emphasis increasingly has been on cost.

Critics, including patients, doctors and some outside observers, say the result has been to deny patients needed care in some cases. "Obviously, you can cut costs by cutting services," says George Annas, a professor of health law at Boston University, "but that wasn't the idea."

Managed-care health plans do take credit for helping hold down costs, but they insist that the quality of care has not suffered. "I don't know of many physicians who are devoted more to controlling costs than to care delivering," says AAHP President Ignagni.

Access to specialists is the most frequent source of friction between patients and health plans. Health plans control costs by limiting the number of specialists in the plan and the number of referrals to specialists outside the plan; they may pay their primary physicians in ways that create incentives to minimize the number of referrals. For patients, those incentives may create minor burdens — for example, a woman's need to get a referral for routine obstetric care — or more serious disputes.

Critics say the industry has been

States Where Patients Get Special Treatment

Specialist care — *At least thirty states make it easier for people in managed-care health plans to see certain specialists; all but Kentucky allow women either to designate an obstetrician-gynecologist as their primary-care provider or see an ob-gyn without a referral:*

> Alabama, Arkansas*, California, Colorado, Connecticut, Delaware, Florida**, Georgia***, Idaho, Illinois, Indiana, Kentucky****, Louisiana, Maine*****, Maryland, Minnesota, Missouri, Mississippi, Montana, Nevada, New Jersey, New Mexico, New York, North Carolina, Oregon, Rhode Island, Texas, Utah, Virginia and Washington

External review — *Eleven states allow health-care patients to appeal coverage decisions to outside bodies:*

> Arizona, California, Connecticut, Florida, Minnesota, Missouri, New Jersey, Rhode Island, Texas, New Mexico and Vermont

Post-mastectomy care — *Thirteen states require coverage of post-mastectomy inpatient care:*

> Arkansas, Connecticut, Florida, Illinois, Maine, Montana, New Jersey, New Mexico, New York, North Carolina, Oklahoma, Rhode Island and Texas

Gag-rule ban — *Thirty-six states bar insurers from limiting doctors' communications with patients about treatment options:*

> Arkansas, California, Colorado, Connecticut, Delaware, Florida, Georgia, Idaho, Illinois, Indiana, Kansas, Maine, Maryland, Massachusetts, Minnesota, Missouri, Montana, Nebraska, Nevada, New Hampshire, New Jersey, New Mexico, New York, North Carolina, Ohio, Oklahoma, Oregon, Rhode Island, South Carolina, Tennessee, Texas, Utah, Vermont, Virginia, Washington and Wyoming

* also covers optometrist or ophthalmologist; ** also covers chiropractor, podiatrist, dermatologist; *** also covers dermatologist; **** only covers chiropractor; ***** also covers nurse-practitioner, nurse-midwife

Sources: American Association of Health Plans, National Conference of State Legislatures.

physician and network of specialists — actually simplifies decisions for patients. "Unlike the old days, where you went to the phone book, now you have the ability to seek care through a network of professionals working together," Ignagni says.

Moreover, she points out that many plans in recent years have given consumers more options — for example, "point-of-service" (POS) plans that allow enrollees to see physicians outside the plan's network if they pay part of the cost through a higher deductible or a percentage of the fee. "We recognize that [a closed-plan HMO] doesn't meet the needs of all consumers," she says, "and that's why these other products have been developed."

Still, state and federal legislators are seeking ways to assure patients easier access to specialists. Some 30 states require health plans to give women the option of selecting an obstetrician as their primary-care provider. *(See table, at left.)* A number of states are considering bills to establish a procedure for a "standing referral" to a specialist for patients with chronic or life-threatening diseases or conditions. In Congress, Norwood and a number of other lawmakers have endorsed similar provisions.

Annas says health plans should be required to pay specialists whenever a subscriber must go outside the network. "I don't think that would happen very often," he says. "But it's not really a health plan if it doesn't offer the full range of medical services."

Norwood's bill, as well as some bills in the states, also includes a provision requiring health plans to offer a "point-of-service" option. Some critics say that would harm patients by undercutting the ability of HMOs to control costs and reduce premiums.

"The way HMOs keep costs down is by hiring physicians who practice conservatively" and don't order a lot of tests, says John Goodman, president of the National Center for Policy

making it more difficult for health-plan subscribers to see specialists. "Managed-care plans are increasingly using payment systems that discourage providers from referring patients to specialized care," John Seffrin, president of the American Cancer Society and chairman of the National

Health Council, told the president's patients' rights commission last year.

"For the patient, it is difficult to know what they need to do" to see a specialist, agrees Weinberg, the council's president.

Industry officials, however, say that managed care — with its "gatekeeper"

Analysis, a free-market think tank in Dallas. "You can lower your premiums by joining an HMO that employs doctors who practice conservative medicine. If you take away the HMO's ability to do that, you take away one of the options that people have."

For their part, industry officials argue against any regulatory requirements, saying that market forces will drive health plans to give patients more choices for getting to a doctor of their choice. "Many plans are moving in that direction," Gradison says. "The question is whether the law should require that in every case, and my answer would be no."

But Paul Starr, a professor of sociology at Princeton University and author of a well-regarded history of the medical profession, says the industry cannot be counted on to give patients adequate choices for health care.

"We need legislation because whatever they're doing today doesn't guarantee what they'll do tomorrow," says Starr, who was an adviser for President Clinton's unsuccessful national health-care initiative in 1993 and '94. "They can just as easily withdraw access as provide it."

Should health plans be subject to medical malpractice liability?

When Ron Henderson died in a Kaiser Permanente hospital in Dallas in 1995, his family sued the HMO and several of its doctors for not diagnosing his heart disease.

Kaiser denied any wrongdoing and depicted Henderson as an overweight smoker who had ignored doctors' instructions. But the family's lawyers turned up embarrassing evidence of Kaiser's efforts to control costs by limiting hospital admissions in cardiac cases. In December 1997, Kaiser settled the case for $5.3 million. [4]

Kaiser was subject to a malpractice suit because, unlike most HMOs, it directly employs the physicians and nurses in its clinics. Courts have held that HMOs that contract with individual doctors or medical groups are shielded from malpractice suits on the theory that the doctor rather than the health plan is actually providing the care. But a new Texas law seeks to erase that distinction. [5]

"I can see no reason why a private, very profitable enterprise ought not be held accountable for mistakes that are made when everybody else is," says Texas state Sen. David Sibley, a conservative Republican and oral surgeon.

The new Texas law, which took effect on Sept. 1, was strongly pushed by the state medical association but vigorously opposed by health insurers. Geoff Wurtzel, executive director of the Texas HMO Association, called the law "bad policy" and blamed its enactment on what he termed "medical politics."

"In 1995, the Legislature overwhelmingly agreed that the threat of being sued didn't produce a better standard of care," Wurtzel said, referring to a restrictive malpractice law passed that year. "But all of a sudden, if it was HMOs, liability was OK."

Texas was the only state to directly subject health plans to malpractice liability. But Missouri opened the door to malpractice suits against HMOs by repealing a law that gave health plans a defense against malpractice. And Rhode Island and Washington, among others, have created commissions to study the issue.

The Texas law was challenged in federal court by the Aetna insurance company on the grounds that it is pre-empted by the federal law that governs employee benefits, including health insurance.

That law — known as ERISA, short for the Employee Retirement Income Security Act — is also now at the center of the legislative debate in Congress. Reform bills such as the one proposed by Norwood and Dingell would provide that ERISA does not pre-empt state laws dealing with malpractice liability, as some federal courts have held. Those courts have held that health-plan subscribers who feel they were wrongly denied medical care can sue the plans only for reimbursement of the value of the care they did not receive. [6]

Norwood says there is no justification for shielding health plans from malpractice suits. "If you're a health-plan accountant or administrator and you want to make decisions about medical necessity," Norwood explains, "then you have to be responsible about those decisions in a court of law."

The AMA, a strong supporter of limiting medical malpractice suits in the past, supports the change. "When I make a decision, I as a physician accept accountability and liability," says Reardon. "When the plan makes a decision to provide or not to provide treatment, they should have the same responsibility and liability, especially when they're overriding a recommendation from the treating physician."

But the health insurance industry is adamantly opposed. "That's a perfect example of raising the costs of insurance with little, if any, discernible effect on the quality of the care," says the HIAA's Gradison. "It's a boon for the trial lawyers; I don't think it's a boon for the patients at all."

"All of the data suggest that consumers are not the beneficiaries of the current system," says AAHP President Ignagni. "We don't do families very much good if we provide them in the end with a situation that is designed to maybe provide compensation, maybe not, vs. trying to set up a situation that is built on quality improvement in which injuries don't occur in the first place."

One patients' group voices a similar interest in improving medical care without resorting to litigation. "We feel [litigation] is not necessarily the most productive way to resolve problems," says Weinberg of the National Health Council. Instead, Weinberg

The Downside to Managed Care

A majority of Americans believe health maintenance organizations (HMOs) and other managed-care plans have had some adverse effects on health care, according to a 1997 survey. Overall, though, two-thirds of the respondents in managed care gave their plans an A or B, compared with three-fourths of the people with traditional health insurance coverage.

Percent of Americans who say HMOs and other managed-care plans have . . .

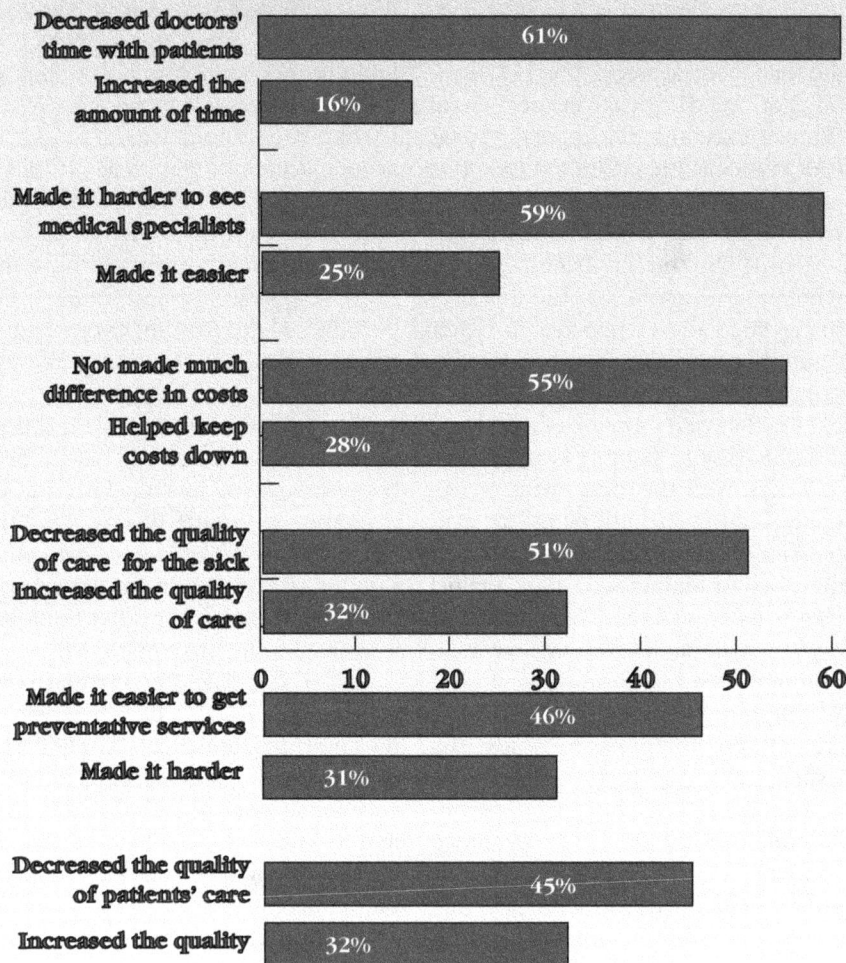

Decreased doctors' time with patients	61%
Increased the amount of time	16%
Made it harder to see medical specialists	59%
Made it easier	25%
Not made much difference in costs	55%
Helped keep costs down	28%
Decreased the quality of care for the sick	51%
Increased the quality of care	32%
Made it easier to get preventative services	46%
Made it harder	31%
Decreased the quality of patients' care	45%
Increased the quality	32%

Note: Percentages do not add up to 100 because "No effect" and "Don't know" responses are not shown.

Source: "Kaiser/Harvard National Survey of Americans' Views on Managed Care," November 1997.

says her group favors strong complaint-resolution procedures, such as the use of ombudsmen.

Other consumer groups go further and call for some independent external review of treatment decisions. "When a patient is denied coverage, it's ludicrous to think that they can appeal to the same system that denied them," says Mitchem of Consumers Union. But her group also favors malpractice liability for health insurers. "We want to ensure that there's some type of remedy that consumers can have access to," she says.

Health insurers are balking at any requirement for outside review procedures. "Some plans are doing this," Gradison says. "The question is whether it should be required by law."

Experts differ sharply on the potential effects of subjecting HMOs to malpractice liability. "If you apply tort liability to HMOs, you'll force them to do things that are not cost-effective," Goodman says. "You'll force them to waste money."

But Barry Furrow, a professor of health law at Widener University School of Law in Wilmington, Del., says that the threat of liability would result in better medical care by forcing managed-care administrators to focus more on quality than on costs. "You want to shift the competition more away from price and toward quality," Furrow says.

Are stronger safeguards needed to protect the privacy of patients' medical records and information?

The ongoing transformation from a paper-based health-care system to one that relies on electronic records has spawned an intense debate over who has access to individuals' medical histories and whether the information could be used to deny employment or health insurance. Recent cases of identity theft, hacker attacks on commercial Internet sites and more innocent technological snafus have reinforced a perception that personal information is not secure.

The Department of Health and Human Services (HHS) was expected at the end of 2000 to release guidelines that will allow government agencies, law enforcement and government researchers expanded access to medical databases. The guidelines stem from the Health Insurance Portability and Accountability Act of 1996, which, among other things, mandated Congress to develop national medical privacy standards by August 1999. When lawmakers missed the deadline, the task fell to HHS, which says its standards also will address consumer rights to see medical records and outline penalties for violating patient privacy. Privacy groups, such as the Andover, Mass.-based Coalition for Patients' Rights, say the draft rules will not give patients any meaningful control over their medical histories and may allow doctors, insurers and other parties to share information without prior consent.

An early Clinton administration patient-privacy proposal, developed in 1997, spends nearly 40 pages detailing and justifying exceptions to the general rule prohibiting disclosure of patient records without the patient's consent. The list includes exceptions to disclose information necessary for the patient's health care, for payment and for internal oversight of the patient's treatment. The recommendation also calls for permitting disclosure of individually identifiable information to public health authorities for "disease or injury reporting, public health surveillance or public health investigation or intervention."

Most controversially, the administration also said that law enforcement or intelligence agencies should be able to obtain such information, without a court order, if needed for

"a legitimate law enforcement inquiry" or — in the case of intelligence agencies — if needed for "a lawful purpose."

HHS Secretary Donna E. Shalala disputed advance reports that the proposal broadened law enforcement access to patient information. [7] She said the provision simply restated existing law. But Sen. Tim Hutchinson, an Arkansas Republican, said the proposal gave patients less privacy than existing federal law for bank records, cable television and video store rentals. Sen. Patrick J. Leahy of Vermont, the committee's ranking Democrat, was also critical. "There is divided opinion in the administration," Leahy said, "and right now the anti-privacy forces are winning on the key issue of law enforcement access to medical records." [8]

"HHS completely dropped the ball" on the issue, says Georgetown's Gostin. "They made an unforgivable mistake."

Gostin also faulted the privacy recommendations from the president's commission, issued two months after Shalala's testimony on Capitol Hill. The report called for permitting disclosure of patient information for purposes of "provision of health care, payment of services, peer review, health promotion, disease management and quality assurance." It addressed law enforcement only obliquely, saying law enforcement agencies "should examine their existing policies to ensure that they access individually identifiable information only when absolutely necessary."

"Everybody's in favor of privacy," Gostin says. "But the devil's in the details, and these don't provide any details. It basically does nothing."

For their part, however, health industry and business groups saw the administration's proposals as unduly restrictive. "The industry is very concerned about interrupting the flow of health information," said Heidi

Wagner Hayduk, a consultant on privacy issues for the Healthcare Leadership Council, a coalition of major insurers, hospitals and drug companies. Medical innovation would be "stifled," she warned, if health-care providers and researchers were required to obtain patient authorization "every time information changes hands." [9]

Health-care industry groups also said federal legislation should pre-empt any state laws setting stricter protections for patient privacy. The administration's proposal would leave state laws unaffected, as would a stricter bill introduced by Leahy. But Sen. Robert F. Bennett, a Utah Republican, has introduced a bill that would set a single federal standard on the issue.

The administration also has endorsed a separate privacy proposal affecting the health insurance industry: a bill to bar health insurance companies and managed-care plans from discriminating against people on the basis of their genetic make-up. [10] The proposal has been pushed by a number of bioethics and privacy-advocacy groups, which point to studies documenting instances of genetic discrimination by, among others, employers and insurers.

The genetic privacy bill has languished in Congress for several years. Vice President Al Gore announced the administration's support for also banning genetic discrimination in the workplace. [11]

The administration's medical-records privacy proposal drew additional criticism at a second Senate Labor Committee hearing on the issue. Two medical groups, the AMA and the American Psychiatric Association, both called for stronger protection than the administration supported, while witnesses representing drug manufacturers and the American Hospital Association said the proposal went too far.

Such praise as the administration received for its proposal has been typically begrudging, at best. Boston University's Annas says the administration deserved credit for proposing a federal law guaranteeing patients the right to see their own records. And Robert Gellman, a privacy consultant who led Shalala's outside advisers on the recommendations, stressed that the package would be "stronger than any comparable state law." [12] But both men also faulted the law enforcement provisions, among other exceptions. "The administration," Annas concludes, "has a long way to go." ∎

BACKGROUND

Health Insurance

Health care became widely available to most Americans, and a financially secure profession for most doctors, only in the recent past. [13] Well into the 20th century, routine health care was a luxury available only to well-to-do Americans. And many doctors had only modest incomes, since they did not see enough patients often enough to have a lucrative practice.

Two 20th-century developments changed the face of health care in the United States: widespread private health insurance and government-funded medical programs. Together, the two developments produced the mythic image that forms the backdrop of today's debate over medical care. In that idealized vision, most Americans enjoyed the services of a family doctor, a Marcus Welby figure who gave skilled and compassionate care from birth to death with little concern about fees. And the government stepped in to provide care for those few who could not afford medical services. But the two developments also contained the germs of the cost problems that beset the health-care system today.

Private insurance entered the health field tentatively, limited at first to covering accidental injury and death. By the late 19th and early 20th centuries, however, many employers were providing limited medical care for their workers — motivated as much to reduce absenteeism caused by illnesses as to promote their employees' welfare.

The labor scarcities of World War II prompted some employers to begin offering health insurance as a benefit for workers. Labor unions, strengthened by New Deal legislation in the 1930s, included demands for health benefits in contract negotiations. And the postwar economic boom allowed major U.S. corporations to grant the demands.

Through the 1950s, more and more big corporations were including health benefits in union contracts; other employers followed suit. By the end of the decade, around two-thirds of the population at least had hospitalization insurance. [14]

The bill for these benefits was largely invisible. The expense was not a big cost item for employers, at least initially. For employees, the benefits were not taxed: In fact, the amounts did not even appear on pay stubs. As a result, many critics and observers contend, no one — neither business, labor, insurers nor health-care providers — had much incentive to watch the bottom line.

A second problem — access to care — was also somewhat obscured. With so many Americans sharing in the widened availability of health care, it was easy to overlook those who were not: the elderly, the poor and the uninsured.

Government's Role

The government's initial moves to help provide health care were also tentative and limited. Some local governments began including medical benefits for the poor in general welfare programs in the early 20th century, and a New Deal program helped bring health care to some rural areas during the Depression. Throughout the century, progressives and labor interests called for compulsory national health insurance, but the efforts were blocked by business interests and, most important, the medical profession.

The two big federal health programs, Medicare and Medicaid, were enacted over the continuing opposition of the medical profession in the brief moment of liberal triumph in the 1960s. Congress had passed a limited bill to provide health insurance for the elderly poor in 1960, but the program proved to be unpopular. President Lyndon B. Johnson put the issue of health care for the elderly at the top of his Great Society agenda and pushed legislation through the overwhelmingly Democratic Congress in 1965.

As enacted, Medicare included the original idea of a contributory insurance program to cover hospitalization for the elderly (Part A) plus a similar plan for doctors' services (Part B). In addition, the law established the framework for Medicaid, the federal-state health-care program for the poor and the disabled.

Some doctors talked of boycotting Medicare, but they quickly realized that the program was — as Starr writes — "a bonanza," guaranteeing payment for medical services that

Chronology

Before 1950

Earliest forms of managed care are organized; employers begin to offer hospitalization insurance to workers.

1960s

Federal government establishes free health insurance for the elderly (Medicare) and a joint state-federal program to provide health care for low-income persons (Medicaid).

1970s

The Nixon administration backs the creation of health maintenance organizations (HMOs) to control health-care costs.

1973
The Health Maintenance Organization Act provides funds and regulatory support for HMOs, but also includes some coverage mandates that slow their growth.

1976
Congress eases some regulations on HMOs; two years later, Congress votes increased funding.

1980s

HMOs grow rapidly, gaining support from employers and consumers worried about spiraling increases in health-care costs.

1985
Supreme Court rules that Employee Retirement Income Security Act (ERISA) supersedes state laws regulating private employers' health plans *(Massachusetts Mutual Life Insurance Co. v. Russell)*; some lower federal courts interpret decision as barring malpractice suits against managed-care plans.

1990s

Backlash against managed care grows.

1993
President Clinton proposes National Health Security Act, aimed at providing health insurance for all Americans; plan is assailed by business interests, medical lobby and Republicans.

1994
Clinton health-care plan dies in Congress.

1995
Many states pass laws requiring managed-care plans to allow women to designate ob-gyns as their primary-care provider.

Aug. 21, 1996
Clinton signs law making it easier for people to keep their health insurance when they lose or change jobs, start their own business or get sick; bill includes provision to facilitate sharing of patient information among health-care providers, but also requires government to develop privacy-protection guidelines by 1999.

September 1996
Congress responds to criticism of "drive-through deliveries" by requiring health insurance plans to cover at least 48 hours of hospital care for new mothers.

May 1997
Texas enacts legislation subjecting health maintenance organizations to medical malpractice liability; Aetna insurance company challenges law in federal court as pre-empted by ERISA.

July 1997
House and Senate conferees agree on provision in budget bill to bar Medicare-eligible HMOs from imposing "gag rules" on doctors by preventing them from discussing treatments or specialists that the plan would not pay for.

Sept. 11, 1997
Health and Human Services Secretary Donna E. Shalala presents medical-information privacy legislation to Congress; proposal is faulted by lawmakers, advocates and experts.

October 1997
Two House subcommittees hold hearings on Patient Access to Responsible Care Act sponsored by Rep. Charlie Norwood, R-Ga.

Nov. 19, 1997
Proposed "Patients' Bill of Rights" is issued by President Clinton's Advisory Commission on Consumer Protection and Quality in the Health Care Industry.

January 1998
Managed-care plans continued to grow in 1997 despite complaints about their services; coalition of health insurance and business lobbies announces plans for advertising campaign against managed-care reform legislation; Clinton urges Congress to pass consumer bill of rights.

June 2000
Supreme Court rules patients cannot sue managed-care plans for malpractice under ERISA.

Are Elderly Americans "Trapped" by Medicare?

awmakers and rival interest groups are clashing over the ability of senior citizens to see the physician of their choice outside the federal Medicare system. [1]

Conservatives want to get rid of a policy that largely prevents doctors and patients from arranging for Medicare-covered services outside the system's reimbursement scheme. They view the issue as a simple question of patients' rights.

"When you're sick, the federal government should not stand in the way of your getting the medical treatment you want," says Sen. Jon Kyl, an Arizona Republican who took up the issue after a constituent's complaint last year and forced a limited amendment to the law through Congress.

But the Clinton administration, Democratic lawmakers and the nation's largest senior citizens' group all argue that totally lifting the restriction would create the risk of gouging senior citizens and threaten the viability of the federal government's 33-year-old health insurance program for the elderly.

Seniors "would lose much of the financial protection that they are currently provided under Medicare" if the policy were eliminated, according to Rep. Pete Stark, a California Democrat and veteran legislator on health-care issues.

The dispute stems from a policy adopted by the Health Care Financing Administration (HCFA), the Health and Human Services agency that administers the Medicare program. For many years, the HCFA has prohibited doctors participating in the Medicare program from letting patients pay them out of their own pockets for services covered by Medicare.

Defenders of the policy say Medicare is acting just like any other insurer by requiring participating doctors to limit their fees to its schedule for reimbursements. Medicare reimbursements are sometimes markedly lower than prevailing fees for some services.

"Private payment would undermine the whole rationale for the Medicare fee schedule," says John Rother, legislative director of the American Association of Retired Persons (AARP). The 30-million-member organization strongly opposes lifting the ban.

Critics say the ban is bad for senior citizens and also bad for the Medicare program. They say it prevents senior citizens who can afford it from picking a particular doctor, for example, or from getting treatment without going through government red tape.

As for Medicare itself, these critics say that letting well-off seniors pay for some services themselves would strengthen the financially beleaguered insurance program. Supporters counter that lifting the ban would result in a two-tiered system — with one group of doctors for well-to-do seniors and another for Medicare patients.

Kyl won Senate passage on a party-line vote of an amendment to narrow the policy last summer as part of the Medicare reform provisions of the balanced-budget bill. [2] But the Clinton administration reportedly threatened to veto the entire bill over the issue. The result was a limited compromise that allows physicians to accept private payments for Medicare-covered services if they "opt out" of the Medicare program for two years. Critics say that few doctors could afford to drop out of the Medicare program.

A conservative senior citizens' organization is challenging that law in federal court in Washington. [3] United Seniors Association, a 60,000-member group founded in 1992, claims the law violates senior citizens' constitutional rights.

United Seniors President Sandra Butler says the new law makes health care less accessible for senior citizens. "Because seniors will be barred from contracting privately, many health- and life-saving services will be difficult for them to obtain, if they could obtain them at all," Butler says.

But Rother says few seniors agree. "I don't think I have a single letter in my file asking for the privilege of paying more for the services that Medicare already covers," he says. "This is not a patient-driven concern."

Medical groups are also divided on the issue. The American Medical Association (AMA) strongly supports Kyl's effort this year to repeal the restriction on private payments. "Medicare patients deserve the same rights as other patients to purchase health care directly from their physicians — without interference from the federal government," the AMA says.

But the American College of Physicians, which represents about 100,000 internists, opposes Kyl's bill. It says the measure "could threaten the viability of Medicare as an insurance program that offers accessible, affordable high-quality care."

---

[1] For background, see *USA Today*, Nov. 26, 1997, p. A6 and "Retiree Health Benefits," *The CQ Researcher*, Dec. 6, 1991, pp. 930-953.

[2] See *Congressional Quarterly Weekly Report*, June 28, 1997, p. 1529.

[3] The case is *United Seniors Association v. Shalala*, pending before U.S. District Judge Thomas F. Hogan.

many doctors had previously provided for free or for reduced fees. [15] Medicare and Medicaid closed the biggest gaps in health-care access, but liberals still said health care was too costly and favored broader national health insurance to ensure access for all.

Under President Richard M. Nixon, however, the federal government took a different tack to deal with the intertwined issue of access and costs. It backed a free-enterprise solution to the problems: a scheme being pushed by a physician-turned-health-care reformer in Minnesota that came to be called a "health maintenance organization" or HMO.

Rise of Managed Care

Managed care had its origins in ideas pushed by socially conscious health-care reformers in the early 20th century. [16] In one form — known as cooperative or prepaid group health plans — consumers paid a modest annual fee to one or more doctors to cover their families' preventive and sick care. The medical profession opposed the idea, however, and succeeded in getting laws passed in many states to bar consumer-controlled cooperatives.

Then during World War II, California industrialist Henry J. Kaiser set up two prepaid group health plans for his company's employees, known as Permanente Foundations. Unlike the health-care cooperatives, Kaiser's plans flourished — and served as the forerunner for what is today the country's largest HMO, Kaiser Permanente.

The Nixon administration saw in HMOs an appealing alternative to the liberal-backed national health insurance plans. Administration officials were sold on the idea by Paul M. Ellwood, today regarded as the father of managed care. Ellwood, a Minneapolis physician, argued that the traditional fee-for-services system penalized health-care providers who returned patients to health. He met with the administration's key health policy-makers on Feb. 5, 1970, to make his case for organizations to provide members comprehensive care for prepaid amounts. At that meeting Ellwood coined the phrase "health maintenance organizations." [17]

Financial and regulatory help were needed to put the idea into effect. The administration initially found money to help launch HMOs beginning in 1970, without specific congressional authorization, even as it was asking Congress to pass a law to promote the plans. The law enacted three years later — the Health Maintenance Organization Act of 1973 — provided more money, $375 million over five years, for grants and loans to help start up HMOs. [18] More important, the law required all businesses with more than 25 employees to offer at least one HMO as an alternative to conventional insurance if one was available.

At the same time, though, the act established requirements that proved to be regulatory obstacles to the growth of HMOs. It required HMOs to offer not only basic hospitalization, physicians' services, emergency care and laboratory and diagnostic services but also mental health care, home health services and referral services for alcohol and drug abuse.

These requirements, combined with the government's delay in promulgating regulations to implement the law, stunted the growth of HMOs, according to Starr's account. At the same time, the medical profession viewed the idea with skepticism or hostility. But Congress eased some of the burdens in 1976, and then provided another shot of money in 1978: $164 million over three years. [19] By then, HMOs were starting to take off in the market. At the end of the decade, HMOs had enrolled 7.9 million members — double the figure in 1970. Still, the number represented only 4 percent of the population and — as of the early 1980s — was expected to grow only to 10 percent of the population by 1990. [20]

In fact, enrollment in HMOs more than tripled over the next decade, reaching about 25 million in 1990. Despite a decade of rapidly rising health-care costs, HMOs had to keep fees down and provide good service in order to attract customers. Most faced business losses, and some went bankrupt. But they were generally regarded as successful in containing cost increases, enough so that traditional fee-for-service health plans began copying some of their practices, such as utilization review, where insurers scrutinized doctors' fees and practices.

Meanwhile, the once comfortable relationship between patients and doctors had become badly frayed. The growth of specialized medicine had weakened the bond with the old-style family doctors — who now likely as not called themselves "internists." The rise in doctors' income created a distance between an increasingly well-to-do profession and its patient-customers. And the increase in malpractice litigation led many physicians to adopt "defensive-medicine" practices to guard against the threat.

Managed-Care Backlash

The 1990s saw managed care reach a dominant position in the health insurance market. By 1993, most workers covered by employer-provided health insurance were enrolled in some form of managed care — either an HMO, a preferred provider organization (PPO) or a "point-of-service" (POS) plan. As of 1995, industry figures estimated a total of 150 million people nationwide were in a managed-care plan. Managed care was also credited with helping to bring down the rate of increase in health-care costs. But the decade also witnessed a growing backlash against managed care as many doctors chafed under cost-cutting pressures from HMO administrators, and many patients complained of delays in receiving — or outright denials of — needed medical care.

The consumer backlash against HMOs manifested itself most dramatically in court. A small number of HMO enrollees won whopping verdicts or settlements in suits claiming that their health plans had wrongfully denied or delayed necessary medical care. In California, the family of Helene Fox, who died of breast cancer after her HMO, Health Net, refused to pay for a bone marrow transplant, collected a $5 million settlement after a jury awarded her $89 million. In Georgia, Lamona and James Adams won a $45 million jury award in a suit that blamed Kaiser Permanente for the botched handling of a bacterial infection that forced doctors to amputate their infant son's arms and legs; the company later settled for an undisclosed sum. [21]

A mid-decade survey produced statistical evidence of the consumer dissatisfaction with HMOs, at least in comparison with traditional fee-for-service health plans. The survey, conducted for the Robert Wood Johnson Foundation by researchers at Harvard University and Louis Harris and Associates, found that significantly more HMO subscribers than fee-for-service plan subscribers complained about their medical care.

The complaints came only from small minorities: For example, 12 percent of HMO subscribers said their doctors provided incorrect or inappropriate medical care, compared with 5 percent of fee-for-service plan subscribers. Still, the higher levels of dissatisfaction with HMOs prompted a cautionary note from the survey's director. "Consumers need to be aware that all health plans don't treat you the same way when you are sick," said Robert Blendon, chairman of the department of health policy management at Harvard's School of Public Health. [22]

Health-care providers were also voicing dissatisfaction with managed care. In one incident, Massachusetts internist David Himmelstein attacked the HMO that he worked for, U.S. Healthcare, in an appearance on Phil Donahue's nationally syndicated television program in November 1995.

Himmelstein charged that the company rewarded doctors for denying care and forbade them from discussing treatment options with patients. The company — later acquired by Aetna — responded by terminating its contract with Himmelstein just three days after the TV show. But it reinstated him in February 1996 after a storm of criticism and also modified its contracts to permit doctors to discuss payment methods with patients.

Himmelstein's comments reflected the concerns that many doctors and hospital administrators had about managed care. "This is all about cost, not improving patient care," a doctor told *Wall Street Journal* reporter George Anders in a 1994 interview. "You survive in managed care by denying or limiting care," William Speck, chief executive of Presbyterian Hospital in New York, told Anders in June 1995. "That's how you make money." [23]

As the complaints escalated, state and federal lawmakers took up the issues. By mid-decade, hundreds of bills were being introduced in state legislatures around the country. The earliest legislation dealt with specific problems — like allowing women to select an ob-gyn physician as their primary-care provider, or prohibiting health-care plans from imposing "gag clauses" on physicians. Congress in 1996 passed a provision requiring health insurance plans to cover at least 48 hours of hospital care for new mothers — prohibiting so-called "drive-through maternity stays." [24]

Lawmakers also have responded to the growth of Medicare managed care. By the end of 1999, an estimated 6.3 million Medicare beneficiaries, or about 16 percent, were enrolled in some variety of managed-care plan, instead of in a traditional fee-for-service program. The Medicare managed-care option was viewed as attractive by some, because the plans could cover services that the traditional Medicare program

would not, most notably prescription drugs. A program called Medicare+ Choice, approved by Congress in 1997 as part of the Balanced Budget Act, allows beneficiaries to choose a managed-care plan that provides all health services for a monthly fee that is set by the Medicare program and sometimes supplemented by a small premium from the beneficiary.

While Medicare+Choice was promoted as a potential boom in health care, the program went into turmoil in the fall of 1998, when health plans — faced with lower-than-expected reimbursements from Medicare — withdrew from the program. Forty-three major health plans quit the program in 1999, in a move that affected some 415,000 seniors, and left 45,000 of them with no managed-care option at all. Another 41 plans left in 2000, affecting about 327,000 beneficiaries. Analysts believe such pullouts will continue in regions where the plans determine they cannot make a sufficient profit. But lawmakers are divided on whether reimbursement rates should be adjusted to reflect higher medical costs, and, if so, by how much. ∎

CURRENT SITUATION

Reform Efforts

A June 2000 U.S. Supreme Court decision on patients' rights to sue their health plans clarified one important aspect of the debate over managed-care overhaul, but did little to resolve political differences.

Justices in *Pegram v. Herdrich* ruled that a patient cannot sue a health plan under the Employee Retirement Income Security Act of 1974 (ERISA) because the plan offered bonuses to physicians to hold down costs. Justices said a decision in a patient's favor would have undermined the fundamental structure of the managed-care system, adding that it is up to Congress, not the courts, to set guidelines for insurers and patients. "The federal judiciary would be acting contrary to the congressional policy of allowing (health maintenance) organizations if it were to entertain (a) claim portending wholesale attacks on existing HMOs solely because of their structure," wrote Justice David H. Souter.

The suit stemmed from a claim by a Bloomington, Ill. woman, Cynthia Herdrich, that her physician, Lori Pegram, compromised her treatment in 1991 after she complained of abdominal pain. Instead of immediately sending Herdrich for a diagnostic ultrasound at a nearby clinic, Pegram scheduled the test for eight days later at a less expensive clinic 50 miles away. During the delay, Herdrich's appendix burst. During oral arguments in February 2000, Herdrich's attorney tried to convince justices that they should expand the right of patients to sue under ERISA by allowing Herdrich to claim Pegram failed to meet her duties as a trustee who controlled her health plan's administration of benefits.

The case was closely watched because ERISA — a law primarily designed to protect workers' pension rights — has long been criticized as a liability shield for health insurers. Most courts have held that an individual injured by an ERISA denial of care can only sue in federal court, and then only to recover the cost of the denied benefit and assorted court costs. The high court, in denying the right to sue, explored several other legal possibilities. In a lengthy footnote to the ruling, justices indicated

Managed-Care Reforms Get Qualified Support

Most Americans support several of the frequently mentioned proposals to make managed care more user-friendly. But their support drops when they are asked to consider potential consequences of the changes such as higher premiums.

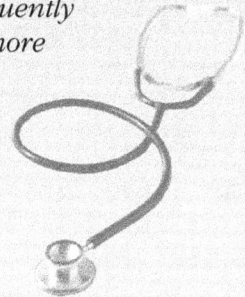

Percentage of Americans who want health plans to . . .

	Favor	Oppose
Provide more information about how health plans operate	**92%**	**6%**
If higher premiums result	58%	34%
If the government gets too involved	55%	38%
If employers drop coverage	54%	43%
Allow appeal to an independent reviewer	**88%**	**9%**
If higher premiums result	63%	32%
If the government gets too involved	51%	41%
If employers drop coverage	49%	45%
Allow a woman to see a gynecologist without a referral	**82%**	**16%**
If higher premiums result	63%	34%
If the government gets too involved	51%	43%
If employers drop coverage	48%	47%
Allow people to see a specialist without a referral	**81%**	**18%**
If higher premiums result	58%	39%
If the government gets too involved	47%	48%
If employers drop coverage	46%	51%
Pay for an emergency room visit without prior approval	**79%**	**18%**
If higher premiums result	62%	33%
If the government gets too involved	52%	41%
If employers drop coverage	48%	47%
Allow people to sue health plan directly	**64%**	**31%**
If higher premiums result	58%	34%
If the government gets too involved	55%	38%
If employers drop coverage	54%	43%

Note: Percentages do not add up to 100 because all respondents did not answer.

Source: Kaiser/Harvard "National Survey of Americans' Views on Managed Care," January 1998.

that health plans may have a responsibility to disclose details about coverage decisions to their patients — a move that could lead to class-action lawsuits claiming the plans breached their ERISA responsibilities by failing to tell patients about their financial structure.

The decision did little to settle a long-running impasse between congressional Democrats and Republicans over managed-care overhaul. Discussions to merge House and Senate bills fell apart in mid-2000 precisely over the issue of a patient's right to sue and how employers might be liable for an insurer's decision about medical care. However, in an indication of the increased political potency of the issue, Senate Republicans in June 2000 went on record in favor of expanding patients' rights to sue, in limited circumstances, during a vote on an amendment to the fiscal 2001 Labor, Health and Human Services and Education appropriations bill. The move, which came in response to a rival Democratic amendment designed to embarrass the GOP on the issue by making them appear to be protecting insurers, endorsed a limited right to sue managed-care plans for damages — an issue Senate Republicans staunchly opposed when the Senate considered and passed a managed-care bill in 1999.

The concession would allow lawsuits against managed-care companies in two instances: unreasonable delays in essential medical care and the failure to cover treatment that an independent physician deemed necessary and said the plan should cover. Patients could not win punitive damages, but could recover unlimited economic damages and as much as $350,000 for pain and suffering. But GOP and Democratic lawmakers continued to disagree over who should be covered by the new rules. The new proposal would limit most

protections to the approximately 56 million Americans in self-insured health plans that are not covered by state patient protection laws. Democrats and some House Republicans who support the Norwood-Dingell managed-care overhaul bill want broader protections and want the lawsuits to be handled in state courts, not federal courts. They also oppose the $350,000 cap on non-economic damages.

The Senate vote was not enough to revive stalled House-Senate talks on a managed-care overhaul bill. The House-passed provision combined the Norwood-Dingell measure with separate legislation featuring so-called "access" provisions that many Republicans believe will give more people affordable coverage. The provisions include an expansion of a pilot program for medical savings accounts (tax-exempt accounts used for medical expenses) and the creation of insurance-purchasing groups, which supporters believe will allow people to get health coverage for more affordable rates. Many Democrats were skeptical of the provisions, saying they doubted the proposals would reduce the ranks of the uninsured. The House provision also would allow patients to sue in state courts for damages. Health plans would be protected from punitive damages if they passed an external review. The House measure notably would cover all 191 million privately insured Americans.

Disagreements between Democrats and Republicans — and between House and Senate Republicans — doomed prospects for a compromise. Lawmakers said there was the possibility of reviving the measures in the 107th Congress, particularly with Democrats picking up seats and pressing for more health-related legislation.

Norwood says he introduced the original managed-care bill despite his

aversion to federal regulation. "It turns my stomach to turn this over to the Labor Department," he said, referring to the agency that would have principal responsibility for implementing the bill's provisions. "But it makes me even more nervous not to do anything."

Among its major provisions, Norwood's bill would require health plans to give consumers an option to buy "point-of-service" coverage — allowing them to select their own doctor for an additional cost. It would also require adequate access to specialists and emergency care, require internal grievance procedures and subject managed-care companies to medical malpractice liability for negligent treatment decisions.

Despite professed support from a majority of the House, Republican leadership remains unenthusiastic. House Majority Leader Dick Armey of Texas as far back as 1998 wrote a strongly worded letter to GOP members urging opposition to the forthcoming recommendations from President Clinton's health-care commission. Even though Armey did not refer to Norwood's bill, he called for restricting rather than expanding medical malpractice liability and recommended medical savings accounts rather than regulatory changes to give consumers more health-care choices. [25]

For its part, the health insurance industry is gearing up for an all-out lobbying campaign to defeat Norwood's bill or anything much like it. "It's our No. 1 issue," says HIAA's Gradison. "It's very bad public policy."

In a two-page lobbying flier, the AAHP warns that Norwood's bill would represent "the single, largest expansion of tort liability in memory," establish "federal price controls" and make it harder for families to get "affordable" health coverage. But Ignagni also hints at the possibility of supporting some legislative changes. "We intend to be very involved and will provide whatever information that we can," she says.

At Issue:

Has the rise of managed care hurt patients' rights?

ADRIENNE MITCHEM
Legislative counsel, Consumers Union

*a*mericans are experiencing a true crisis in confidence in today's managed-care industry. Consumers' faith is shaken because of signs that managed care may be sacrificing quality health care to boost profits.

As managed care replaced the old fee-for-service system, the financial incentives driving the health-care industry have turned upside down. This revolution, replacing incentives to overtreat patients with incentives to undertreat, has provoked a strong backlash. Nearly three in five Americans in a recent poll believe managed-care plans make it harder for people who are sick to see a specialist.

But this revolution also creates an opportunity to reintroduce a simple and old-fashioned idea: consumer protection laws. Responding to grass-roots uprisings, states have passed laws giving consumers tools to help them be smart shoppers, ensure accountability when costly mistakes are made, provide more access to specialist and emergency care and guarantee a fair system to review patient disputes.

A presidential advisory commission has developed a "Consumer Bill of Rights," spurring a flurry of bill introductions on Capitol Hill and the promise of a healthy debate about nationwide reform. On one side is a multimillion-dollar scare campaign, funded by industry, designed to preserve the status quo. On the other, a coalition of consumer groups and individual Americans who have been burned by the current system and want change.

A scorecard of principles for reform from Consumers Union will help measure who wins:

• The linchpin for consumers is an appeals system that gives patients access to an independent entity to settle disputes over medically necessary care when benefits are denied, terminated or delayed. The current system, where the managed-care company serves as both judge and jury for every appeal, is stacked against patients.

• Another vital component is full disclosure. Plans should be required to provide consumers with information to help them understand all of their alternatives for treatment, not just the cheapest.

• Consumers also want assurance that they will not be holding the bag for medical mistakes. Families shouldn't shoulder the financial burdens of medical negligence because industry is unaccountable for its actions.

• Finally, a consumer bill of rights should set minimum standards for all managed-care plans. Voluntary provisions won't suffice. When you get sick, doctors, not accountants, should call the shots.

Congress can restore consumer confidence in the managed-care system by passing enforceable and loophole-free legislation that includes a fair review process, full disclosure and accountability. Anything less falls short of true reform.

KAREN IGNAGNI
President, American Association of Health Plans

*h*ealth plans have advanced the cause of patients' rights with important patient protections that weren't available under the old system. Health-care practices and procedures have been made far more accountable — ensuring that the great majority of patients get the right care, at the right time and in the right setting — and appeals systems are in place to make sure that any patient who disagrees with a coverage or treatment decision has effective recourse.

Discussions of patients' rights should start with the fact that, from a patient's perspective, all other rights are meaningless without access to care. Under the old system, health care was being priced beyond reach. So one of the most important victories that health plans have won for patients' rights is to make health coverage more affordable for millions of working Americans.

Once assured of coverage, you should have the right to be protected against inappropriate care. Health plans promote quality care by emphasizing prevention and early diagnosis and monitoring practice patterns in order to do away with the wide variations in quality that did so much to make the old system not just costly but often downright dangerous. This commitment to accountability represents a major advance in patient protection.

But what if a conflict arises about what's covered or whether a particular treatment is in order? Despite critics' claims, disputes are rare and are usually resolved satisfactorily. Still, there's room for improvement — and health plans are participating in a nationwide initiative to continually improve care by identifying consumer concerns and developing patient-centered solutions. This, too, represents an unprecedented commitment to patients' rights.

Consumers should be wary of much that is being touted today as "consumer protection." For example, efforts to make health plans liable for individual practitioners' actions would simply clog the courts (at taxpayer expense) and enrich trial lawyers (not patients). At the same time, such efforts would adversely affect care by forcing health plans to act defensively, causing higher costs without producing better outcomes. Does that protect patients' rights? No — it just turns back the clock.

And we can't afford that. The health-care revolution that's in progress today was a necessary answer to the costly flaws of the old system. If the revolution has imperfections, the answer is to correct them — not to roll back progress or micromanage plans. Health plans are fully committed to making sure consumers are informed and their concerns met. That way, we can protect patients' rights without smothering innovative health care under layers of inflexible regulations and unproductive litigation.

Estimated Costs of Reform Vary Widely

Two studies — one funded by an industry group, the other by a patient-consumer coalition — reached dramatically different conclusions about the likely cost impact of the original and most widely supported managed-care reform proposal in Congress. But the industry's substantially higher estimate depends on interpretations of the bill, the Patient Access to Responsible Care Act (PARCA), that its sponsor says are wrong.

A report prepared for the insurance-business Health Benefits Coalition by the Washington consulting firm of Milliman & Robertson projected the bill would raise health insurance premiums by 23 percent.[1]

A study prepared for the Patient Access to Responsible Care Alliance — also known as PARCA — by Muse & Associates predicted a rate increase of between 0.7 to 2.6 percent.[2]

The reports made strikingly similar predictions about the effects of some provisions. Both reports, for example, predict little if any effect from provisions requiring emergency care coverage, easing referrals to specialists or giving consumers a choice between types of managed-care plans.

The industry-funded study, however, predicted substantially higher costs for three provisions in the bill:

• No payments to providers as an inducement to reduce or limit medically necessary services. Milliman & Robertson assumed the provision would prevent health plans from negotiating discount rates with providers and projected a 9.5 percent cost increase as a result. Muse & Associates noted that newly drafted report language specifically denied any intention to bar discounts; on that basis, it predicted no cost impact. Difference: 9.5 percent.

• Equal reimbursement for out-of-network providers. Milliman & Robertson say the provision could have no impact if interpreted to apply only to doctors' fees, but could raise premiums by 11 percent if it prevented point-of-service (POS) plans from requiring enrollees to pay a higher deductible for using an out-of-network provider. The firm then averaged the two figures to produce a "best estimate midpoint" of 5.5 percent. Muse & Associates says

the bill would not bar higher deductibles for using a doctor outside the network. Difference: 5.5 percent.

• No discrimination against health professionals. Milliman & Robertson says the provision could require health plans to cover services of professionals not now covered, such as chiropractors or acupuncturists. Muse & Associates said new report language stipulates the bill will not have that effect. Difference: 5.5 percent.

In addition, the industry-funded study predicted that because of its projected increases, some customers would drop their coverage — raising rates still further for consumers still in plans. The consumer-funded study predicts a much smaller effect. Difference: 4.5 percent.[3]

The Muse study predicted only a slight increase from a provision subjecting group health plans to medical malpractice liability; the Milliman-Robertson study did not analyze the provision.

Milliman & Robertson qualified its study by stating that several of its projections "depend heavily on interpretation of PARCA." For its part, Muse & Associates noted that its study took account of legislative changes made after the Milliman & Robertson study was completed.

Rep. Charlie Norwood, R-Ga., the main sponsor of PARCA, says the industry-funded study is based on a misreading of his bill. "The assumptions made are neither reasonable nor honest," he says.

But the Health Benefits Coalition, the business group that released the study, is standing by its predictions. "We have other studies that show that mandates at the state level have raised rates," a spokeswoman says, "and we expect federal regulation to be even more costly."

---

[1] Milliman & Robertson Inc., "Actuarial Analysis of the Patient Access to Responsible Care Act (PARCA)," released Jan. 21, 1998.

[2] Muse & Associates, "The Health Premium Impact of H.R. 1415/S.644, the Patient Access to Responsible Care Act (PARCA)," Jan. 29, 1998.

[3] Milliman & Robertson says its individual cost estimates total more than its "composite" prediction of 23 percent because some PARCA provisions overlap.

OUTLOOK

Weighing the Costs

The intense partisanship and narrow margins facing the 107th Congress make it difficult to predict whether any managed-care reform proposals will be enacted into law. Health-insurance groups such as AAHP and HIAA along with big-business lobbies such as the U.S. Chamber of Commerce and National Federation of Independent Businesses continue to argue that sweeping reforms would be bad medicine for patients. Specifically, they say legislation giving patients the expanded right to sue managed-care plans for health decisions will drive up premiums and force some small businesses to drop health insurance coverage for their employees.

Norwood and other reform advocates say such arguments are to be expected. "This is pretty normal,"

Norwood says. "The insurance companies stay in the background and try to push the Chamber of Commerce into the front. Yes, that will be formidable opposition. The problem is that they don't have the people on their side, and we do."

Indeed, studies show the public increasingly supports many provisions included in managed-care bills in Congress and in state legislatures. One 1998 survey by the Kaiser Family Foundation and Harvard University found substantial majorities in favor of such proposals as allowing people to appeal to an independent reviewer, to see a specialist or to sue health plans directly. (See poll, p. 55.)

The survey also indicated, however, that public support for those ideas drops significantly if people are asked about the consequences forecast by opponents, such as higher premiums, and reduced health-insurance coverage. "Support may fall if the public comes to see (the proposals) as part of a larger government health-reform plan that could result in employers dropping coverage of higher health insurance premiums," says Drew Altman, president of the Kaiser Family Foundation. Many of the major companies in the industry have been very profitable during the past decade, but in 1997 some of the biggest — including Kaiser, Aetna and Oxford Health Plans Inc. — reported losses. [26] The pressure on the industry has eased somewhat because of the slowing pace of health-care inflation. Managed-care companies also are finding other places to cut costs — for instance, dropping out of the Medicare program in areas where reimbursements lag far behind actual costs of treatment.

Even so, some insurers are beginning to raise premiums in anticipation of accelerating increases in health-care costs over the new few years. [27] Many of the price hikes are

linked to the flood of expensive new drugs hitting the market. The cost debate will turn in part on which side managed to convince the public and lawmakers that it has "credible experts" on its side, experts say. The debate already has produced dueling studies on the issue. (See story, p. 58.) One study prepared for the insurance industry and a coalition of business groups projected a 23 percent increase in health insurance premiums if Norwood's proposal were enacted. A rival study for the Patient Access to Responsible Care Alliance forecast a "slight increase" in managed-care premiums of from 0.7 to 2.6 percent. [28]

In Minnesota, however, Dianne Shea believes that the debate over patients' rights should not turn on costs. "This is the richest country in the world, and we're arguing about how to provide health care for everyone," she says. "Isn't it the right of every American to have health care?"

"We've come up with a solution to every problem in this country," Shea concludes. "I know we can come up with a way to provide good health care to people." ∎

Notes

[1] The American Association of Health Plans reported that nearly 150 million Americans belonged to managed-care plans at the end of 1995, the most recent year surveyed: 58.2 million in HMOs and 91 million in preferred provider organizations (PPOs). See "1995 AAHP HMO and PPO Trends Report." An annual survey of employer-provided health-benefit plans released last month shows that the percentage of employees enrolled in managed-care plans rose in 1996 and 1997. See Mercer/Foster Higgins "National Survey of Employer-Sponsored Health Plans." In his State of the Union address on Jan. 27, President Clinton said that 160 million Americans are in managed-care plans today.

FOR MORE INFORMATION

American Association of Health Plans, 1129 20th St., N.W., Suite 600, Washington, D.C. 20036; (202) 778-3200; www.aahp.org. The trade association represents health maintenance organizations (HMOs) and similar network health-care plans.

American Medical Association, 1101 Vermont Ave., N.W., 12th Floor, Washington, D.C. 20005; (202) 789-7400; www.ama-assn.org. The AMA, with 300,000 members, is the nation's largest physicians' group; it supports some managed-care reform proposals.

Consumers Union of the United States, 1666 Connecticut Ave., N.W., Suite 310, Washington, D.C. 20009; (202) 462-6262; www.consumersunion.org. Consumers Union, publisher of Consumer's Report, lobbies on health issues in Washington and in state capitals.

Health Benefits Coalition, 600 Maryland Ave., S.W., Washington, D.C. 20004; (202) 554-9000. The ad hoc coalition, comprising 31 business trade associations, opposes managed-care reform bills in Congress.

Health Insurance Association of America, 555 13th St., N.W., Suite 600E, Washington, D.C. 20004; (202) 824-1600; www.hiaa.org. This trade association represents 250 of the country's major for-profit health insurance carriers.

Patient Access to Responsible Care Alliance, 1111 14th St., N.W., Suite 1100, Washington, D.C. 20005; (202) 898-2400. The ad hoc coalition of 70 patient, provider and consumer-advocacy groups supports the major managed-care reform bill in Congress — the Patient Access to Responsible Care Act (PARCA).

[2] The 8th U.S. Circuit Court of Appeals ruled on Feb. 26, 1997, in *Shea v. Esensten* that the suit could proceed. The court ruled that Shea could sue her HMO under the federal benefits protection law known as ERISA for failing to disclose its system for reimbursing doctors.

[3] For background, see "Managed Care," *The CQ Researcher*, April 12, 1996, pp. 313-336.

[4] See *The Dallas Morning News*, Dec. 23, 1997, p. 1C and *The Washington Post*, Dec. 20, 1997, p. D1.

[5] For background on the debate over medical malpractice litigation, see "Too Many Lawsuits," *The CQ Researcher*, May 22, 1992, pp. 433-456.

[6] For background, see Barry R. Furrow, "Managed Care Organizations and Patient Injury: Rethinking Liability," *Georgia Law Review*, Vol. 31, winter 1997, pp. 419-509, and Clark C. Havighurst, "Making Health Plans Accountable for the Quality of Care," *ibid.*, pp. 587-647.

[7] See *The New York Times*, Sept. 10, 1997, p. A1.

[8] See *The New York Times*, Sept. 12, 1997, p. A24.

[9] PBS, "The NewsHour With Jim Lehrer," Sept. 16, 1997.

[10] For background, see "Medical Screening Raises Privacy Concerns," *The CQ Researcher*, Nov. 19, 1993, p. 1023. For opposing views on the issue, see *USA Today*, April 19, 1996, p. 13A.

[11] See *USA Today*, Jan. 20, 1998, p. 1A.

[12] Quoted in *The Washington Post*, Sept. 12, 1997, p. A1.

[13] Some background is drawn from Paul Starr, *The Social Transformation of American Medicine: The Rise of a Sovereign Profession and the Making of a Vast Industry* (1982).

[14] See *ibid.*, p. 334.

[15] *Ibid.*, pp. 369-370.

[16] Some of this material can also be found in "Managed Care," *The CQ Researcher*, April 12, 1996, pp. 324-327.

[17] Starr, *op. cit.*, p. 395.

[18] See 1973 *Congressional Quarterly Almanac*, pp. 499-507.

[19] See 1976 *Congressional Quarterly Almanac*, pp. 544-548, and 1978 *Congressional Quarterly Almanac*, pp. 576-580.

[20] Starr, *op. cit.*, p. 415.

[21] Details of the Fox and Adams case, along with citations to contemporaneous news accounts, can be found in George Anders, *Health Against Wealth: HMOs and the Breakdown of Medical Trust* (1996). Health Net had argued in the Fox case that the bone marrow transplant was not covered because it was an experimental procedure; Kaiser contended that it provided proper care in the Adams case.

[22] See "Sick People in Managed Care Have Difficulty Getting Services and Treatment," Robert Wood Johnson Foundation, June 28, 1995.

[23] Anders, *op. cit.*, pp. 42, 47.

[24] See 1996 *Congressional Quarterly Almanac*, pp. 10-85. The provision was included in the fiscal 1997 appropriations bill for the Veterans Administration, Department of Housing and Urban Development and other agencies. For a critical view of the impact of the law, see *Newsweek*, Aug. 4, 1997, p. 65.

[25] For background, see *Congressional Quarterly Weekly Report*, Nov. 22, 1997, pp. 2909-2911.

[26] See *The Wall Street Journal*, Dec. 22, 1997, p. A1 (Kaiser) and *The Washington Post*, Jan. 4, 1998 (Aetna, Oxford).

[27] See *The New York Times*, Jan. 11, 1998, p. A1.

[28] Milliman & Robertson, Inc., "Actuarial Analysis of the Patient Access to Responsible Care Act (PARCA)," released Jan. 21, 1998; Muse & Associates, "The Health Premium Impact of H.R. 1415/S.644, the Patient Access to Responsible Care Act (PARCA)," Jan. 29, 1998.

Bibliography

Selected Sources Used

Books

Anders, George, *Health Against Wealth: HMOs and the Breakdown of Medical Trust*, Houghton Mifflin, 1996.

Anders, a reporter for *The Wall Street Journal*, provides a strongly written, critical account of the impact of health maintenance organizations on patients' rights. The book includes detailed source notes.

Annas, George J., *The Rights of Patients: The Basic ACLU Guide to Patient Rights* [2d ed.], Humana Press, 1989.

This American Civil Liberties Union handbook, updated in 1989, gives an overview of patients' rights in such areas as informed consent, medical records, privacy and confidentiality and medical malpractice. The book includes source notes and an eight-page list of organizations and other references. Annas is a professor of health law at Boston University's schools of medicine and public health.

Goodman, John C., and Gerald L. Musgrave, *Patient Power: Solving America's Health Care Crisis*, Cato Institute, 1992.

Goodman and Musgrave argue strongly that the country's health-care "crisis" calls for free-market solutions — reducing government regulation, diminishing the role of insurance and giving individual consumers and patients greater responsibility for paying for their health care. Goodman is president of the National Center for Policy Analysis, a free-market think tank in Dallas; Musgrave is president of Economics America Inc., a consulting firm in Ann Arbor, Mich.

Patel, Kent, and Mark E. Rushefsky, *Health Care Policies and Policy in America*, M.E. Sharpe, 1995.

The book gives an overview of contemporary health-care issues. It also includes a brief chronology (1798-1995) and a 23-page bibliography. Patel and Rushefsky are professors of political science at Southwest Missouri State University.

Starr, Paul, *The Social Transformation of American Medicine: The Rise of a Sovereign Profession and the Making of a Vast Industry*, Basic Books, 1982.

This widely praised study traces the history of the U.S. medical profession and health-care system from the 1700s through the birth and emerging growth of managed care in the 1970s and early '80s. Starr, a professor of sociology at Princeton University, has been an adviser to President Clinton on health-care policy. The book includes detailed source notes.

White, Joseph, *Competing Solutions: American Health Care Proposals and International Experience*, Brookings Institution, 1995.

White compares the U.S. health-care system with those in other countries, including Australia, Canada, France, Germany, Great Britain and Japan. He is a research associate in governmental studies at the Brookings Institution.

Articles:

Langdon, Steve, "Critics Want More 'Management' of Managed Care Industry," *Congressional Quarterly Weekly Report*, March 15, 1997, pp. 633-640.

The article provides an overview of legislative developments on managed care at the start of the 105th Congress, along with summaries of major bills, legislative activity in selected states and a glossary.

Reports and Studies

Advisory Commission on Consumer Protection and Quality in the Health Care Industry, *Consumer Bill of Rights and Responsibilities: Report to the President of the United States*, November 1997.

The 72-page report by the 34-member commission appointed by President Clinton contains recommendations dealing with such issues as choice of providers and health plans, complaints and appeals and confidentiality of health information. A list of references and selected reading are included.

Computer Science and Telecommunications Board, National Research Council, *For the Record: Protecting Electronic Health Information*, National Academy Press, 1997.

This book-length report details a scientific panel's findings and recommendations on protections for electronic health information. The book includes an 11-page bibliography as well as detailed source notes.

Kaiser Family Foundation/Harvard University, *National Survey of Americans' Views on Managed Care*, Nov. 5, 1997; *National Survey of Americans' Views on Consumer Protections in Managed Care*, Jan. 21, 1998.

The first survey found that majorities of the public are concerned about key aspects of managed health care. The second found majority support for many of the major reform proposals currently being debated, but support dropped when people were asked about potential consequences of changes, such as higher insurance premiums.

Critics Want More 'Management' Of Managed Care Industry

By Steve Langdon

Though Republicans reluctant to impose regulation,
Democrats seize on issue in response to consumer pressures

The managed care industry is under siege. Consumers, unhappy with their health care, are pressuring lawmakers to regulate health maintenance organizations and other so-called managed care insurance plans. The accusation: These companies are putting profits before patients.

Washington has taken notice. Congressional Democrats have seized the issue, introducing a wide array of bills, some comprehensive and others targeted at more specific problems. Last year, Congress enacted a "drive through delivery" bill (PL 104-204), which requires insurers to cover minimum hospital stays for mothers and their newborns. This year, Republicans also have filed bills to expand coverage and protect patients.

But for all the issue's appeal, the prospect of imposing more regulations on managed care providers is unappealing to the majority Republicans in Congress. Since coming to power in 1995, the GOP has worked to wash away regulations, not write more. Moreover, Republicans are not convinced that the industry cannot regulate itself. The managed care industry, whose health plans generally provide more benefits at lower costs than traditional fee-for-service health plans, already has started a "putting patients first" campaign.

Now Republicans must decide how to defend their anti-regulatory principles while appearing receptive to voters' call for action. If they ignore the issue, it could haunt them in the 1998 congressional campaigns. With the stakes so high, they are moving cautiously. The House and Senate committees with jurisdiction over managed care are taking different tacks. The House Commerce Committee may work on a narrow bill. Senate Labor and Human Resources Committee Chairman James M. Jeffords, R-Vt., may draft comprehensive managed care legislation in late spring or early summer, but it will be less regulatory than some Democrats would like.

Meanwhile, President Clinton has been sluggish to respond. He has imposed new requirements on managed care providers serving patients under Medicare and Medicaid, the federal health insurance programs for the elderly, poor and disabled. But he has done little about the private insurance market. On Sept. 5, he issued an executive order creating a commission to study managed care and related matters, but he has yet to name anyone to serve on it. The panel is supposed to file a preliminary report in just six months.

The managed care debate in Congress will focus on the government's role in the marketplace and in protecting consumers. It may also rekindle the partisan fire that scorched the health care debate of 1994 and the Medicare wars of the last election campaign. Voters, patients and the managed care industry will be watching lawmakers closely.

Strength in Numbers

One of the first prepaid medical practices—as health maintenance organizations (HMOs) were formerly known—was created in Washington state before World War I, according to a 1985 article in the *New England Journal of Medicine*. Drs. Thomas Curran and James Yocum contracted with the lumber industry in 1910 to cover employee health care for 50 cents per member per month.

From *CQ Weekly*, March 15, 1997.

Decades later, rising medical costs prompted President Richard M. Nixon to urge Congress to spur the development of HMOs with federal funds. In 1973, Congress enacted a law (PL 93-222) that defined HMOs and provided $375 million over five years to help study and start them. By the mid-1980s, businesses increasingly turned to HMOs because they charged lower premiums than traditional insurance plans.

What has put managed care on Congress' radar screen again are numbers—large ones. In 1995, 149 million Americans were enrolled in one of two types of managed care plans—HMOs and preferred provider organizations (PPOs)—according to the American Association of Health Plans, which represents 1,000 managed care plans. And the growth is explosive.

The 1995 estimate represented a 15 percent increase over 1994's 130 million. By comparison, there are 38 million enrollees in Medicare, a population considered one of the most powerful constituencies in American politics.

Public relations tactics in the high stakes contest over managed care approach the emotional decibel level of the abortion debate. While anti-abortion activists hand out photographs of aborted fetuses, managed care industry opponents tell stories of dying cancer patients denied care.

A 1996 cover story in *Time* magazine, "What Your Doctor Can't Tell You," profiled a mother of two in her mid-30's fighting with her managed care insurer to cover expensive treatments for breast cancer that had spread to other parts of her body. She died in 1995 before the story was published. And a 45-page report on managed care legislation in the states, called "States to the Rescue," produced by the consumer group Families USA, tells the story of a man who severed his thumb but could not have surgery for three hours because the hospital could not find an HMO-approved surgeon.

Congress has responded to some consumer complaints. Last year, it enacted what was commonly called the "baby bill" or the "drive-through-delivery" bill, sponsored by Sen. Bill Bradley, D-N.J. Many Republicans, including members of the Senate leadership, vigorously opposed the legislation. But they found it hard to fight a measure pitched as protecting motherhood and babies because they were trying to eschew the "extremist" label that Democrats had stuck on them.

Comprehensive Approach

Democrats hope the same pressures from consumers will dominate again. "There's a lot of anxiety out there," says Edward M. Kennedy of Massachusetts, ranking Democrat on the Senate Labor and Human Resources Committee. "I'm confident we'll get legislation."

Kennedy has introduced a comprehensive managed care bill (S 353), and John D. Dingell of Michigan, the ranking Democrat on the House Commerce Committee, has introduced a companion bill (HR 820).

Kennedy called the legislation a "needed response to the surging growth of managed care and the rapid changes taking place in the health insurance market—changes that too often put insurance industry profits ahead of patients' health needs." He provided a litany of problems with managed care practices he hopes his bill will correct. The Kennedy-Dingell bill would:

- Prohibit a health plan from denying coverage for emergency room care if a "prudent layperson" would consider the situation an emergency;
- Require health plans to permit women to use an obstetrician-gynecologist as their primary care doctor;

continues

- Mandate that health plans allow patients with serious illnesses to see doctors and receive treatment outside the plan at no extra cost if the plan does not have the doctors or facilities needed, including treatment in a clinical trial;
- Require plans to report to the public and state agencies on mortality rates, demographics, disenrollment statistics and other information related to quality of service;
- Require plans to have clear guidelines, administered by a doctor, for reviewing requests for treatment by specialists. Plans would have to explain to patients why they were denied such care, and how they can appeal the decision;
- Require plans to set up a two-stage grievance procedure for patients denied coverage or unhappy with the quality of care. The second stage would be administered by a review panel of outside providers and consultants employed by the plan.
- Fund a health insurance ombudsman program at the state level to assist consumers in choosing a health plan and addressing complaints;
- Prohibit plans from restricting what doctors say to their patients, particularly about treatment options;
- Prohibit plans from drawing contracts with doctors that give them incentives to limit medically necessary services.

Kennedy says even if his comprehensive bill cannot succeed, he believes Congress should move ahead on narrower bills. "We shouldn't wait for the comprehensive to go through."

Targeted Approach

Lawmakers in both chambers and both parties have introduced many targeted proposals to regulate managed care plans. Bills dealing with three issues have received the most attention: emergency room coverage, mastectomy coverage and the so-called gag rule prohibition that bans health plans from restricting what doctors can say to their patients.

Rep. Greg Ganske, R-Iowa, a doctor, has been the lead proponent of gag rule legislation. He and Commerce Committee colleague Edward J. Markey, D-Mass., have reintroduced a bill (HR 586) that stalled last year after the Commerce panel approved it.

"When you're lying in a hospital bed very ill, you just have to trust that your doctor is going to tell you all your treatment options . . . not just the cheap ones OK'd by your managed care plan," Ganske said.

The proposal would impose fines up to $25,000 on health plan companies that try to restrict communication between patients and doctors. States would generally enforce the ban; the federal government would enforce it for companies not regulated by states or for companies in states without adequate enforcement. Ganske has more than 190 cosponsors from all over the ideological spectrum.

Because of its long list of cosponsors, the Ganske-Markey bill will probably be approved by the Commerce Committee. But the panel will not hold hearings on broader managed care issues before next month. Panel Republicans and the House leadership are less inclined than their Senate counterparts to move comprehensive managed care legislation this year, according to a senior House GOP aide. "It's sort of amorphous," the aide said. "It's too early to see how all of this is going to play out." But he said it is up to the managed care industry and businesses who fear that government mandates could increase insurance costs to mount a public relations campaign: "If they don't make the case, they're going to lose these kinds of votes."

Another bill with bipartisan backing would prohibit health plans from requiring women undergoing mastectomies to have the surgery on an outpatient basis. Alfonse M. D'Amato of New York, the principal Republican sponsor in the Senate, has lined up ultra-conservative cosponsors such as Lauch Faircloth of North Carolina as well as liberals such as Carol Moseley-Braun, D-Ill.

Other bills address emergency room coverage. Some health plans, after reviewing emergency room treatments, have refused to cover them because they felt the medical situation was not an emergency.

Critics say such a policy discourages people with potentially life-threatening conditions from going to the emergency room. The most often cited example is a person with chest pains who turns out to have heartburn. A layperson cannot tell whether the chest pains are serious. The proposed bills generally require health plans to cover emergency room trips for conditions that a "prudent layperson" might see as an emergency.

While support for managed care legislation has grown in Congress, opposition has solidified, too. Several Republicans who supported the 48-hour maternity stay legislation last year are now cautious about putting more mandates on the industry.

"Last year we fired a shot over the bow with the 48-hour bill," says the Senate's only physician, Bill Frist, R-Tenn., a Labor panel member. "If managed care fails to focus on quality and ignores the patient relationship, the federal government will act." But, he says, "I'm not going to sign on to a laundry list of anti-managed care legislation body part by body part." Frist has not supported gag rule legislation.

Jeffords, the Senate Labor panel's new chief, agrees. "We should not legislate standards for each and every disease or medical procedure," he said at the end of his March 6 managed care hearing. Jeffords, like Kennedy, prefers a comprehensive approach. "Many of the things in there will be attractive to us," he says of Kennedy's bill. But his own bill, which Jeffords says will combine many other proposals, will not give the federal government as much regulatory authority. Jeffords could not steer a Kennedy-style bill through the Senate, even if he wanted to.

Jeffords' priorities include emergency care coverage, gag rules, grievance procedures, establishing accreditation requirements for health plans, and setting up standards for measuring health care quality.

A more general concern of Jeffords' is what some call the "ERISA void," a reference to the intricate and complicated relationship between state and federal insurance regulation. In 1945, Congress enacted a law, the McCarran-Ferguson Act (PL 79-15), that established states as the regulators of insurance. But in 1974, it enacted another law—the Employee Retirement Income Security Act (PL 93-406)—ERISA—which reclaimed some of the federal government's regulatory authority, but only for so-called self-insured companies. A company that self insures is one that accepts the financial risk of an insurance plan instead of paying an insurer to accept it. Large, well-capitalized companies are most likely to be self-insured. Under ERISA, a company that covers its own risk for pension or health plans is considered self-insured and exempt from state regulations.

Jeffords points out that the federal government has rules for regulating self-insured pensions, but few for health insurance. "The federal government has got to step into the ERISA area," he says. "Nobody else has the authority." That is particularly important regarding managed care because more and more self-insured companies are turning to such plans—and there are few regulations protecting their employees, compared with the web of state laws that protect individuals whose companies buy insurance.

In testimony March 6, Kansas insurance Commissioner Kathleen Sebelius explained why she believes Congress needs to regulate self-insured health care plans: "We don't have any other authority to enforce any sort of market standards for self-funded plans." She said she often gets complaints from patients, but cannot help because their company is self-insured. "Who is going to respond to those consumer complaints?" she asked.

continues

Last year's new health laws, including the maternity stay provisions, the health insurance portability bill (PL 104-191) and a measure setting standards for mental health coverage (PL 104-204), were rare instances of Congress enacting federal health insurance laws affecting self-insured plans.

'Putting Patients First'

The consumer group campaigns, the threat of federal regulation and a spate of unfavorable news stories have not fallen on deaf ears in the managed care industry. It has begun to lobby Capitol Hill, warning lawmakers of the dangers of regulation. And it has started a major public relations campaign. "We need to be out front clarifying and explaining what we do," says Karen Ignagni, who heads the American Association of Health Plans. Her group is aggressively seeking to ease concerns about managed health care. The industry is moving fast to demonstrate that it can regulate itself, without federal interference.

At the core of that effort is the association's Putting Patients First plan—an industry policy that addresses many issues targeted by Congress in proposed legislation. To give it teeth, the group's board of directors voted not to renew or grant membership in the association for plans that do not adhere to the policy. "Our members want patients to know what they can expect from their health plans," Ignagni says. "We want to send a clear message that we are listening and taking steps that are in tune with changing needs."

The still-evolving policy includes general guidelines as well as specific rules. For example, the policy states that health plans should:

- Cover emergency room visits for conditions that "reasonably appear to constitute an emergency";
- Expedite patient appeals of decisions to deny coverage;
- Not require outpatient care for a mastectomy, allowing that decision to be made by the doctor and patient.

Ignagni says she has sensed a shift in thinking on Capitol Hill. "More and more members are saying to us that they are very concerned about micromanagement," she says. "I think things are coming together in a way that Congress may step back and re-examine the role of government" in the regulation of managed care.

Clinton's Commission

Ignagni's group favors appointing a government commission to study health care quality issues. Clinton has said he will appoint such a panel, but is still checking potential members' backgrounds, according to the Department of Health and Human Services (HHS). At Jeffords' March 6 hearing, Bruce Fried, director of the Office of Managed Care at the Health Care Financing Administration, said Clinton is "very close" to naming the panel, adding that the Sept. 30 deadline for issuing a preliminary report remains unchanged. A final report is due 18 months after the commission's first meeting.

According to Clinton's Sept. 5 executive order, panel members will include representatives from consumer groups, health care providers, insurers and state and local officials. Though not officially a commission on managed care, its mission statement tracks the issues most often talked about in that context. Broad guidelines in the executive order charge the commission to "advise the president on changes occurring in the health care system and recommend such measures as may be necessary to promote and assure health care quality and value, and protect consumers and workers in the health care system."

Besides creating a commission, the president has given managed care plans doing business with the federal government through Medicare and Medicaid new rules that track what lawmakers have proposed for the private market.

On Feb. 12, the Department of Health and Human Services sent letters to 350 managed care plans that contract with Medicare, prohibiting them from limiting hospital stays for mastectomy patients, or requiring that the surgery be done on an outpatient basis. According to the department, Medicare paid for 84,000 mastectomies in 1996—roughly a third of those done in the United States. The federal government can directly control Medicare and Medicaid providers in ways that it cannot control the private insurance market. It is the nation's largest purchaser of health care, giving it enormous leverage over contractors.

The Clinton administration also imposed a gag rule ban on Medicare and Medicaid managed care providers—even though it said it had no evidence that the problem existed. Also, in March 1996, HHS prohibited such managed care providers from paying doctors to limit needed medical services, and required plans to limit doctors' financial losses when they refer patients to specialists.

Uncertain Future

Sparse lawmaker attendance at the March 6 hearing—limited at times to only Jeffords and Kennedy—suggests that managed care has not caught fire yet. If it does, Congress has many ways to respond. Which option Republicans choose depends on variables that are not yet known. If the GOP perceives the pressure to legislate as temporary, Congress may do nothing or work on a few narrowly targeted bills.

But given that Republicans in both chambers are lead sponsors on several of the narrower bills and are working hard to make them high-profile issues, GOP leaders will find it hard to oppose all managed care legislation with a unified front. And if public pressure mounts and Democrats leverage that anxiety among voters, the GOP may have to consider a more comprehensive approach or craft a message that explains why more regulation is not the answer.

"What's the most politic way of doing this?" asks a GOP Senate leadership aide. "Do we confront each head on or come up with something more comprehensive or more attractive?"

PATIENT POWER

What Are They Hiding?

By Ellyn E. Spragins

Shopping wisely for medical services isn't easy. Just try to compare doctors' success rates. Or try to find out how many people died from in-house infections at your local hospitals. You probably can't. Thanks to a database called Quality Compass, you can sometimes compare how vigorously different HMOs are immunizing children, screening women for breast cancer and treating chronic conditions. About 447 health plans provide performance data to Quality Compass, which tracks 50 to 60 medical services and business practices. But some of the country's largest managed-care companies—including Cigna, Prudential and Humana—are now refusing to let Quality Compass release their numbers publicly. In 1996, 24 health plans asked the managers of the database to seal their records. And by last year the number of plans requesting secrecy had grown to 155. Why should you care? The reason is simple: if you can't choose a health plan on the basis of quality, the plans have less incentive to shine.

Measuring the performance of HMOs is admittedly tricky. The chief problem is counting how many times a plan actually performs a particular service. Health plans with doctors on staff have a relatively easy time because patient records are centrally located. But companies like Prudential, which contract with physicians in unrelated practices, have to rely on whatever records their member physicians can provide. And because doctors are less good at record-keeping than they are at caregiving, they tend to underrepresent the services they provide. One of Prudential's California plans scored nearly 20 percentage points higher on a prenatal-care measure when the company paid to review the charts of its individual patients. "We're delivering the care," says Tony Kotin, Prudential's chief medical officer. "But Quality Compass doesn't explain how data collection can [skew] a plan's performance."

Many other HMOs face the same problem, but they haven't all decided to withhold information. So what's motivating the dropouts? Do they have something to hide? At *Newsweek's* request, the National Committee for Quality Assurance (NCQA), the nonprofit accreditation group that created Quality Compass, studied the performance of two groups of health plans on 20 different quality gauges. The first group consists of 292 health plans that were completely open about their numbers. The second group contains 155 plans that shared data with Quality Compass (to establish nationwide averages and assess their own standing), but refused to let Quality Compass release the information to database users.

The result? In 1998, the disclosers scored significantly better in 18 out of 20 measures, and about the same in two (both involving mental health). The biggest disparities showed up in immunization rates for children and adolescents, eye exams for diabetics and the use of state-of-the-art drugs to treat heart attacks. The plans that shared their numbers sometimes performed poorly, yet those concealing their data almost always lagged behind. For example, the worst-performing disclosers provided follow-up care to 41.3 percent of women members following childbirth, while the worst-performing concealers followed up with just 22.3 percent.

Full disclosure does carry risks. And some plans try to minimize them without completely stiffing consumers. Cigna, whose plans dominated published lists of poor performers in 1997, pulled its scores from public view last year. But the company still shares information privately with employers and

From *Newsweek*, March 1, 1999. Reprinted with permission.

members who request it. Humana, which considers Quality Compass comparisons misleading, won't even share them directly with its members. "They can go to their health-benefits department," says Humana spokesman Greg Donaldson.

Embarrassment is understandable. So is philosophical disagreement. But data-dodging compounds the widespread perception that HMOs put their own interests before their members'. And every time a plan opts to hide its performance, it gets easier for others to do the same. "If nobody has to report," says NCQA president Margaret O'Kane, "I don't know what the future of public accountability for health plans will be."

What's a consumer to do? Ask your company's benefits department if your plan participates publicly in Quality Compass. Or check the Quality Compass Web site (www.ncqa.org) to find out. If your plan is a discloser, you can check its performance by scanning the Web site or calling 888-275-7585. If your plan is hiding its scores, you should ask why. You'd be nervous buying a car from a company that tried to keep you from comparing its safety record with those of competing models. At best, it means the company doesn't respect your intelligence. At worst, it means there's no intelligent reason to choose the company's product.

At Stake in Senate Debate: HMOs' Shield Against Damage Suits

By David S. Hilzenrath

After Richard J. Clarke, a 41-year-old father of four from Haverhill, Mass., went on a drinking binge in 1994 and committed suicide, his widow sued his health insurance plan for wrongful death. She alleged the health plan had refused to pay for a detoxification program after an earlier suicide attempt.

But a judge threw out the case, saying federal law gave the health plan "a shield of immunity."

"The tragic events set forth in Diane Andrews-Clarke's complaint cry out for relief," U.S. District Judge William G. Young wrote in a 1997 decision. "Nevertheless, this court has no choice but to . . . slam the courthouse doors in her face and leave her without any remedy."

Whether patients or their survivors should be able to file such lawsuits will be at the heart of the debate this week as the Senate takes on the long-simmering question of how to regulate managed care.

After years of clamor about the growing power of health maintenance organizations (HMOs) and other cost-cutting insurers, Senate Republicans and Democrats have drafted competing versions of a "Patients' Bill of Rights." The rival plans address a variety of issues, including coverage of emergency room visits, access to medical specialists, and the right to an independent review when a health plan refuses to pay for medical services.

Many states have already tackled these issues, producing a patchwork quilt of inconsistent regulations. But state consumer protections do not help an estimated 48 million Americans whose health plans are exempt from state regulation.

In the Senate, Democratic and Republican proposals differ on such basic points as whether patients' rights should ordinarily apply to people in HMOs—Republicans would defer to the states—and how much power managed-care companies should wield over doctors' decisions. Generally, Democrats are pushing more aggressive and potentially costlier measures.

Nowhere is the partisan split sharper than on the question of lawsuits.

Under a 1974 law called the Employee Retirement Income Security Act (ERISA), an estimated 125 million Americans with employer-sponsored health benefits are for the most part prohibited from suing their health plans in state courts. Suits over coverage decisions must be brought in federal courts, where the health plans are shielded from punitive damages and awards for pain and suffering, lost income and the like. Typically, the only thing plaintiffs can collect, besides legal fees, is the value of the care that was denied.

The ERISA law was written before managed care transformed the way health care is delivered. Then, disputes about coverage decisions typically centered on payment of medical claims after the patient had received the care. Now, managed-care organizations try to influence the way patients are treated, and a decision to deny coverage is more likely to stop the patient from getting the disputed care.

Senate Democrats are fighting to eliminate health plans' "immunity" from damages under ERISA, arguing that they, like other businesses, should be legally accountable for their actions. Senate Republicans say that approach would invite a flood of litigation, driving up premiums and prompting some employers to drop health benefits.

Democrats have sided with an unlikely alliance of physicians and personal injury lawyers, in addition to consumer groups, while Republicans stand with employers and the managed-care industry.

Consumer advocates say the threat of damages would be the strongest deterrent to the kind of penny-pinching that could compromise patient care. If the only thing health plans stand to lose in lit-

---

From the *Washington Post*, July 11, 1999. Reprinted with permission.

igation is the cost of the care they denied, "they have every financial incentive to delay and delay and deny and deny," said Ronald F. Pollack, executive director of Families USA, a consumer group.

The managed-care industry sees it differently. "Our view is that this provision does nothing to help with health care quality . . . but is really much more of a trial lawyers protection provision," said Susan Pisano, spokeswoman for the American Association of Health Plans, an industry group. Much of the managed-care industry has embraced external administrative appeals as a quicker and less oner-ous alternative. In most states, people insured through state and local governments and individual policies have the right to sue for punitive damages, and some have won huge awards.

In 1994, a jury assessed $89.3 million in damages against a California HMO that refused to provide an autologous bone marrow transplant for a breast cancer patient who later died. The case subse-quently was settled for an undisclosed amount.

This year, the widow of David Goodrich, a county prosecutor in San Bernardino, Calif., won a $120.2 million judgment against Aetna U.S. Healthcare of California Inc. A jury found that the insurer breached its responsibility in his treatment for a rare form of stomach cancer. Aetna is appealing.

But big jury verdicts are just part of the potential price of expanding the right to sue, analysts say. The threat of liability could inhibit health plans' efforts to eliminate unnecessary care, analysts say, be-cause it could make them more afraid to say no to doctors and patients.

To be sure, advocates of the right to sue champion it in the belief it would change the way man-aged-care companies do business. "If they were accountable for their conduct, they would never be-have the way they currently behave," said attorney Michael Bidart, who won the $120.2 million judg-ment against Aetna.

In the aftermath of the $89.3 million judgment for California teacher Nelene Fox, many health plans made it easier for patients to get autologous bone marrow transplants, according to the Congressional Budget Office. More recently, scientific research has cast doubt on the benefit of such procedures for women with advanced breast cancer. Permitting more patients to sue over denials of coverage would almost certainly raise health care costs; the question is how much.

Princeton health economist Uwe Reinhardt said that the financial impact is impossible to know, but he suspects it would be profound. "In the end, we're back again to basically the open-ended deal where the individual physician makes a judgment and no one dares question it," he said.

Jeff D. Emerson, former chief executive of NYLCare Health Plans of the Mid-Atlantic, sees a more modest financial effect, though he foresees other unintended consequences. "I'm not going to make the argument that it's going to be a lot of money."

The Congressional Budget Office, which is responsible for predicting the cost of legislation, said on this question "the supporting data are extremely limited or nonexistent." Ultimately, the CBO projects, removing the barrier to liability as Senate Democrats propose would increase premiums by 1.4 percent.

Aetna U.S. Healthcare, one of the largest insurers, shares the view that liability would drive up pre-miums. But currently, "we would charge the same premium to a customer with the ability to sue as we do those who do not have the ability to sue," spokesman Walter J. Cherniak Jr. said.

Why? "Those judgments to date have been a very small component of overall health care costs," Cherniak said.

The House has resisted past efforts to expand the right to sue, and it is not clear when it will return to the subject of managed care. The entire Senate debate may amount to little more than a rehearsal of sound bites for the next campaign.

H.R. 1595

H.R. 1595, which follows, was considered by the U.S. House of Representatives in 1999. Participants in the simulation will research this bill and debate its merits by holding committee hearings and markup sessions. In the final portion of the simulation, the revised, or marked-up, version of this bill will be debated on the House floor. Participants should read the entire bill and identify the ways in which it needs to be changed.

106TH CONGRESS
1ST SESSION

H.R. 1595

IN THE HOUSE OF REPRESENTATIVES

APRIL 28, 1999

Mrs. LOWEY (for herself, Mr. WOLF, Mr. CANADY of Florida, Mr. TOWNS, Mr. CASTLE, Mrs. MORELLA, Mr. WEYGAND, Mr. INSLEE, Mr. ROTHMAN, Mr. BROWN of Ohio, Ms. SCHAKOWSKY, Mr. LAFALCE, Ms. DELAURO, Mr. MARKEY, Mr. DEUTSCH, Mr. WAXMAN, Mr. LANTOS, Mr. CAPUANO, Mr. FORBES, Mr. GILMAN, Mr. CUMMINGS, and Mrs. CAPPS) introduced the following bill; which was referred to the Committee on Transportation and Infrastructure

---

A BILL

To amend title 23, United States Code, to provide for a national standard to prohibit the operation of motor vehicles by individuals under the influence of alcohol.

1   *Be it enacted by the Senate and House of Representatives of the*

2   *United States of America in Congress assembled,*

3   **SECTION 1. SHORT TITLE.**

4   This Act may be cited as the 'Safe and Sober Streets Act of 1999'.

5   **SEC. 2. NATIONAL STANDARD TO PROHIBIT OPERA-**

6   **TION OF MOTOR VEHICLES BY INDIVIDUALS UNDER THE**

7   **INFLUENCE OF ALCOHOL.**

8   (a) IN GENERAL.—Subchapter I of chapter 1 of title 23, United

9   States Code, is amended by adding at the end the following:

10   `Sec. 165. National standard to prohibit the operation of

11   **motor vehicles by individuals under the influence of alcohol**

12   `(a) WITHHOLDING OF APPORTIONMENTS FOR NONCOM-

13   PLIANCE—

14   `(1) FISCAL YEAR 2003—The Secretary shall withhold 5 percent

15   of the amount required to be apportioned to any State under each of

16   paragraphs (1), (3), and (4) of section 104(b) on October 1, 2002, if the

17   State does not meet the requirements of paragraph (3) on such date.

2

1 `(2) THEREAFTER—The Secretary shall withhold 10 percent

2 (including any amounts withheld under paragraph (1)) of the amount

3 required to be apportioned to any State under each of paragraphs (1),

4 (3), and (4) of section 104(b) on October 1, 2003, and on October 1 of

5 each fiscal year thereafter, if the State does not meet the requirements

6 of paragraph (3) on such date.

7 `(3) REQUIREMENTS—A State meets the requirements of this

8 paragraph if the State has enacted and is enforcing a law providing

9 that an individual who has a blood alcohol concentration of 0.08 per-

10 cent or greater while operating a motor vehicle in the State is guilty

11 of driving while intoxicated (or an equivalent offense under the law

12 of the State for operating a motor vehicle after having consumed

13 alcohol).

14 `(b) PERIOD OF AVAILABILITY; EFFECT OF COMPLIANCE

15 AND NONCOMPLIANCE—

16 `(1) PERIOD OF AVAILABILITY OF WITHHELD FUNDS—

17 `(A) FUNDS WITHHELD ON OR BEFORE SEPTEMBER 30,

18 2004—Any funds withheld under subsection (a) from apportionment to

19 any State on or before September 30, 2004, shall remain available

20 until the end of the third fiscal year following the fiscal year for which

21 such funds are authorized to be appropriated.

22 `(B) FUNDS WITHHELD AFTER SEPTEMBER 30, 2004—No

23 funds withheld under this section from apportionment to any State after

24 September 30, 2004, shall be available for apportionment to such State.

25 `(2) APPORTIONMENT OF WITHHELD FUNDS AFTER COM-

26 PLIANCE—If, before the last day of the period for which funds with-

27 held under subsection (a) from apportionment are to remain available

28 for apportionment to a State under paragraph (1)(A), the State meets

29 the requirement of subsection (a)(3), the Secretary shall, on the first

30 day on which the State meets such requirement, apportion to the State

31 the funds withheld under subsection (a) that remain available for ap-

32 portionment to the State.

3

1   '(3) PERIOD OF AVAILABILITY OF SUBSEQUENTLY AP-

2   PORTIONED FUNDS—Any funds apportioned pursuant to para-

3   graph (2) shall remain available for expenditure until the end of the

4   third fiscal year following the fiscal year in which such funds are so ap-

5   portioned.

6   '(4) EFFECT OF NONCOMPLIANCE—If, at the end of the pe-

7   riod for which funds withheld under subsection (a) from apportion-

8   ment are available for apportionment to a State under paragraph (1),

9   the State does not meet the requirement of subsection (a)(3), such

10 funds shall lapse.'.

11   (b) CLERICAL AMENDMENT—The analysis for such subchap-

12 ter is amended by adding at the end the following:

13   '165. National standard to prohibit the operation of motor vehi-

    cles by individuals under the influence of alcohol.'

The Committee

Roster

What follows is the roster of the House Committee on Transportation and Infrastructure of the 107th Congress (2001–2002). H.R. 1595 was assigned to this committee in 1999, but you will play the role of one of the members of the current committee. Members are listed in order of seniority and are grouped by their respective parties. The most senior member of the majority party is referred to as the committee chair and the most senior member of the minority party is referred to as the ranking member.

House Committee on Transportation and Infrastructure, 107th Congress (2001–2002)

Republicans (in order of seniority)

Bud Shuster, Pa.-9 (chairman)
Don Young, Alaska-AL
Thomas E. Petri, Wisc.-6
Sherwood L. Boehlert, N.Y.-23
Howard Coble, N.C.-6
John J. Duncan, Jr., Tenn.-2
Wayne T. Gilchrest, Md.-1
John Stephen Horn, Calif.-38
John L. Mica, Fla.-7
Jack Quinn, N.Y.-30
Vernon J. Ehlers, Mich.-3
Spencer T. Bachus, Ala.-6
Steven C. LaTourette, Ohio-19
Sue W. Kelly, N.Y.-19
Richard H. Baker, La.-6
Charles F. Bass, N.H.-2
Robert W. Ney, Ohio-18
William Asa Hutchinson, Ark.-3
John Cooksey, La.-5
John R. Thune, S.D.-AL
Frank A. LoBiondo, N.J.-2
Jerry Moran, Kan.-1
Don Sherwood, Pa.-10
James DeMint, S.C.-4
Douglas K. Bereuter, Neb.-1
Michael K. Simpson, Idaho-2
Johnny Isakson, Ga.-6
Rob Simmons, Conn.-2
Mike Rogers, Mich.-8
Shelley Moore Capito, W.Va.-2

Democrats (in order of seniority)

James L. Oberstar, Minn.-8 (ranking member)
Nick J. Rahall II, W.Va.-3
Robert A. Borski, Pa.-3
William O. Lipinski, Ill.-5
James A. Traficant Jr., Ohio-17
Peter A. DeFazio, Ore.-4
Bob Clement, Tenn.-5
Jerry F. Costello, Ill.-12
Eleanor Holmes Norton, D.C.-AL
Jerrold Nadler, N.Y.-8
Robert Menendez, N.J.-13
Corrine Brown, Fla.-3
James A. Barcia, Mich.-5
Bob Filner, Calif.-50
Eddie Bernice Johnson, Tex.-30
Frank Mascara, Pa.-20
Gene Taylor, Miss.-5
Juanita Millender-McDonald, Calif.-37
Elijah E. Cummings, Md.-7
Earl Blumenauer, Ore.-3
Max Sandlin, Tex.-1
Ellen O. Tauscher, Calif.-10
Bill Pascrell, Jr., N.J.-8
Leonard L. Boswell, Iowa-3
James P. McGovern, Mass.-3
Tim Holden, Pa.-6
Nick Lampson, Tex.-9
John Baldacci, Maine-2
Robert Marion Berry, Ark.-1
Ronnie Shows, Miss.-4

Mark Steven Kirk, Ill.-10

Henry E. Brown Jr., S.C.-1

Timothy V. Johnson, Ill.-15

Brian D. Kerns, Ind.-7

Dennis R. Rehberg, Mont.-AL

Todd Russell Platts, Pa.-19

Mike Ferguson, N.J.-7

Sam Graves, Mo.-6

C. L. (Butch) Otter, Idaho-1

Mark R. Kennedy, Minn.-2

Brian Baird, Wash.-3

Shelley Berkley, Nev.-1

Dale E. Kildee, Mich.-9

AL = At large.

Witness List

The following witnesses testified for or against H.R. 1595 in hearings before the House Committee on Transportation and Infrastructure. The chair of the committee will choose the order in which they will testify in the simulation. For the text of the testimonies, see http://library.cqpress.com/gia.

Witnesses against the Bill

Richard Berman, American Beverage Institute
National Restaurant Association*

*Although no specific individual from the National Restaurant Association testified against this bill, the position of this organization is included as a guide for developing actual testimony to deliver before the committee.

Witnesses for the Bill

Katherine P. Prescott, Mothers Against Drunk Driving (MADD)
Joan Claybrook, Public Citizen
Philip R. Recht, National Highway Traffic and Safety Administration

Background Materials on H.R. 1595

Participants will find the following background materials on H.R. 1595 useful in familiarizing themselves with the issues dealt with in the bill. These materials detail the history of the issue, related laws that may influence the debate, and the ways in which the legislation could affect elected constituencies.

Drunken Driving

BY KATHY KOCH

THE ISSUES

Betsy Carlson was 22 when a drunken driver hit her. It was 8 o'clock on a November morning in 1977 as she drove to work in Glen Ellyn, Ill. But Carlson, who now walks with a cane, remembers as if it were yesterday.

"I remember the other car coming across the center yellow line and heading straight at me," she recalls.

She was in a coma for a month and a half, and then three months in the hospital learning to walk and talk again. She suffered brain damage, a broken neck, a shattered left knee, a broken jawbone, two broken wrists and multiple other injuries, some not discovered until years later.

The driver who hit her ended up having to take a driver's re-education course. "Remember," Carlson says, "it was the 1970s, and everybody laughed about drunk driving back then."

Since then, American attitudes about drinking and driving have undergone a sea change. The states and federal government have strengthened enforcement, sponsored anti-drunken-driving campaigns and passed tougher laws covering driving while intoxicated (DWI).

All the attention drove drunken-driving deaths to a record low in 1999, when "only" 15,786 people were killed in alcohol-related crashes — a 43 percent drop from drunken-driving death tolls of the early 1980s. At the same time, the percentage of auto fatalities caused by drunken drivers dropped from 57 percent in 1982 to 38 percent last year. [1]

Such unprecedented progress is partly attributable to the public education and lobbying efforts of the highly

From *The CQ Researcher,* Oct. 6, 2000.

MADD National President Millie I. Webb urges Congress to set the national drunken-driving limit at .08 percent, at a rally on Capitol Hill on Sept. 6. Webb's nephew, in photo, and a daughter died in a crash with a drunken driver.

effective grass-roots organization Mothers Against Drunk Drivers (MADD).

But MADD, which celebrates its 20th anniversary this year, says that problems remain. Alcohol-related collisions still kill 43 people a day — the equivalent of two airplane crashes a week, says Brandy Anderson, MADD's director of public policy.

"If two jetliners were crashing every week — week after week — the public outcry would be deafening," she says. "This issue should not get any less attention, especially since it's a completely preventable violent crime."

Alcohol was involved in 2.7 million car crashes in 1998, according to the Centers for Disease Control and Prevention (CDC). Moreover, the CDC says, Americans drink and drive an estimated 123 million times a year. [2]

The costs are enormous, according to the National Highway Transportation Safety Administration (NHTSA). Each drunken-driving fatality costs about $3.2 million in monetary losses — an estimated $45 billion annually — and injuries cost more than $110 billion a year. [3]

Unfortunately, progress in reducing drunk-driving fatalities has slowed. Over the past three years, America's drunken-driving crash rate has leveled off, as the easiest-to-reach drivers —

social drinkers— have gotten the message.

Today, heavy drinkers, alcoholics and repeat offenders are responsible for most drunken driving and most alcohol-related accidents. During weekends, when most drunken driving occurs, very heavy drinkers — those with a blood-alcohol concentration (BAC) 50 percent above the legal limit — are involved in 65 percent of drunken-driving fatalities, according to NHTSA. And up to one-third of all alcohol-related fatalities are caused by drivers with a prior conviction.

In addition, says Julie Rochman of the Insurance Institute for Highway Safety (IIHS), over the past 20 years drunken driving has increased among women, Hispanics and white males ages 21 to 34.

However, alcohol industry groups claim that federal statistics are overstated because NHTSA defines an "alcohol-related" traffic accident as any crash in which the BAC of anyone involved is .01 percent or greater — one-tenth the level at which most states define drunken driving. The government also classifies an accident as alcohol-related regardless of whether the driver, a pedestrian or a passenger was drinking.

The National Beer Wholesalers Association (NBWA) points out that in 1995, while 41 percent of traffic fatalities were classified as "alcohol-related," only 27.9 percent involved legally drunk drivers. "The NBWA believes federal drunk-driving statistics should accurately reflect the true dimensions of the problem," says an NBWA fact sheet.

Rick Berman, general counsel for the American Beverage Institute (ABI) — which represents family restaurant chains, says 10 percent of those included in federal drunken-driving statistics involved drunk pedestrians

Most States Use Weaker Blood-Alcohol Threshold

Motorists in 31 states can be arrested for drunken driving if their blood-alcohol concentration reaches .10 percent. Mothers Against Drunk Driving (MADD) and other groups want state legislatures to drop the level to .08 percent, the threshold in 19 states, the District of Columbia and Puerto Rico.

BAC Level
- .10 Percent
- .08 Percent

Source: Mothers Against Drunk Driving, 2000

who walked in front of a driver. "Did the drivers kill them or did they kill themselves?" he asks.

But emergency room doctors and nurses say drunken driving is grossly underreported, because very few injured intoxicated drivers are arrested once they enter a trauma center.

To get drunken drivers off the roads, the Clinton administration has pushed for a tougher drunken-driving standard nationwide and has set a goal of reducing alcohol-related fatalities to no more than 11,000 by 2005.

That won't be easy, safety advocates say. "The nation is barely making progress," says MADD President Millie I. Webb, herself the victim of a drunken driver. "We need tougher laws that will . . . [drive] down the number of alcohol-related deaths and injuries."

But the alcohol and entertainment industries, as well as defense attorneys and civil liberties groups, stringently oppose some measures proposed for reaching the 11,000 goal.

Berman dismisses the efforts to tighten up the definition of drunken driving as a "DWI jihad" being conducted by "anti-alcohol nannies."

As the warring sides debate the issues, here are some of the questions being asked:

Should states lower the arrest threshold for drunken driving?

The administration and dozens of safety, law-enforcement, health-care and insurance groups say anyone with a BAC of .08 percent or more is too drunk to drive safely.

Nineteen states and the District of Columbia and Puerto Rico have adopted that legal standard, but the rest

define drunken drivers as anyone with a blood alcohol level of .10 percent — the most lenient drunken-driving threshold in the developed world.

"It is time for the U.S. to join the rest of the industrialized world by drawing the line against drunk driving at .08 BAC," says MADD's Webb, noting that even the wine- and beer-producing countries of Germany, France and Italy have lowered their BAC levels to .08 or lower.

In 1998, Congress adopted incentives for states to switch to the stricter standard. But because only two states have done so since then, supporters say the voluntary approach has failed. Instead, they prefer a measure adopted by House and Senate conferees on Oct. 3 that would deduct a portion of federal highway construction funds from states that don't adopt the stricter standard.

NHTSA, MADD and a coalition of safety groups argue that lower BAC levels are needed because:

• Peer-reviewed, scientific studies show that drivers at .08 BAC cannot brake, steer, change lanes, concentrate, monitor speed or react with appropriate skill to drive safely.

• Mature drivers with a .08 to .09 level of intoxication are 11 times more likely to be in a fatal accident than non-drinkers; for young male drivers the risk is 52 times higher.

• The .08 level is reasonable, and is a higher level of intoxication than "social drinking." To reach a .08 BAC, an average-sized man would have to drink more than four beers in an hour on an empty stomach; a woman would have to drink three.

• States adopting the stricter standard saw an average 6 to 8 percent drop in alcohol-related deaths, which would translate into 500 to 600 additional lives saved annually if all states adopted it.

But restaurant and some alcoholic beverage industry groups dispute nearly all of the above arguments for .08 BAC Berman of the ABI says the stricter standard penalizes responsible social drinking. He says a .08 BAC would make it illegal for a 120-pound woman to drink two 6-ounce glasses of wine on an empty stomach over a two-hour period. "Not many would suggest this is alcohol abuse," he says.

Most drivers know their limits and "self-select themselves" out by not driving when they are too impaired, he says. Others can handle a car fine at a .08 BAC, he adds.

Berman contends that because any alcohol consumption affects driving abilities to some extent, lowering the limit to .08 is just the first step toward making it illegal to drive after even a single drink. He notes that several European countries have lowered their BAC limits to .02 to .05 percent.

The ABI and other alcoholic beverage industry groups argue that .08 BAC

laws do not address the biggest causes of drunken-driving deaths — alcoholics, repeat offenders and those who drive at high BAC levels. Because 75 percent of alcohol-related traffic deaths involved BACs of more than .10 percent, adopting .08 BAC laws is "like lowering the speed limit to 50 mph to slow down maniacs who drive at 100 mph," Berman says.

Lowering the BAC also diverts scarce law-enforcement resources away from apprehending those high-BAC drivers, says the National Beer Wholesalers Association (NBWA).

But .08 proponents adamantly dispute critics' claim that the measure would criminalize social drinkers. They are playing "a smoke-and-mirrors game," says MADD's Anderson. "We have plenty of clear, credible, peer-reviewed studies to show that drivers are too impaired to drive at .08."

As for Berman's claim that drivers know when they are too impaired to drive, she points out that about 3,500 people a year are killed by drivers with a BAC below .10. And by lowering the cutoff to .08, more .10 drivers will be arrested, she says, because police usually do not arrest drivers who are at or close to the legal limit.

Meanwhile, other opponents of .08 argue that the Senate action in June infringes on the 21st Amendment, which gives states the authority to regulate licensed beverages. "I don't believe it is the responsibility of the federal government to set these standards," said Sen. Larry E. Craig, R-Idaho, during a Senate Appropriations Committee markup June 13.[4]

But John Moulden, president of the National Commission Against Drunk Driving (NCADD), points out that all states adopted a 21-year-old drinking age law in 1984, at the urging of then-President Ronald Reagan. "Reagan was certainly no slouch when it comes to states' rights," Moulden says. "But he felt that the safety issue overrode states' rights."

Democratic Maryland state lawmaker William Bronrott argues, "This is not a states' rights issue. This is an issue of special interests vs. the public interest."

However, state and local government organizations, highway contractors and the American Automobile Association argue that states should decide how to spend highway safety and construction funds.

Since the Reagan era, says Frank Schafroth, director of state and federal relations for the National Governors' Association, states have grown increasingly opposed to restrictions being imposed on how federal funds are spent in the states. "Plus, the Senate measure would potentially divert a huge amount of money — 10 percent of federal highway funds — from state programs, and divert funds some governors feel are being used more effectively to reduce drunk driving by going after young and underage drinking drivers," he says.

As for the insurance industry, Rochman says insurers don't believe a .08 law is a silver bullet. "It's not our top priority," she says. "We believe the focus should be on effective enforcement of current laws and on repeat offenders and high-BAC drivers."

Should BAC testing be mandatory after auto accidents involving serious injuries?

When drunken-drivers are killed in car crashes, hospitals can release their blood-alcohol levels to police investigators. But if the drivers are only injured and go to a hospital emergency room (ER), their chances of being arrested or even having their BAC levels checked by police are slim to none — even if the accident caused deaths or other injuries. In fact, some studies show as few as 5 percent of injured drunken drivers admitted to trauma centers are ever charged with DWI.[5]

Breath tests are rarely given to injured drivers at the accident scene because an officer's first priorities are getting the injured to a hospital and restor-

Drunkest Drivers Cause Most Deaths

Drivers with a blood-alcohol concentration (BAC) of .11 percent or greater caused three-quarters of the nation's alcohol-related fatal traffic accidents in 1998. The alcoholic-beverage industry argues that lowering the BAC to .08 percent is pointless because drivers at the higher BAC threshold cause most alcohol-related fatalities.

Blood-Alcohol Level of Drivers in Fatal Accidents, 1998

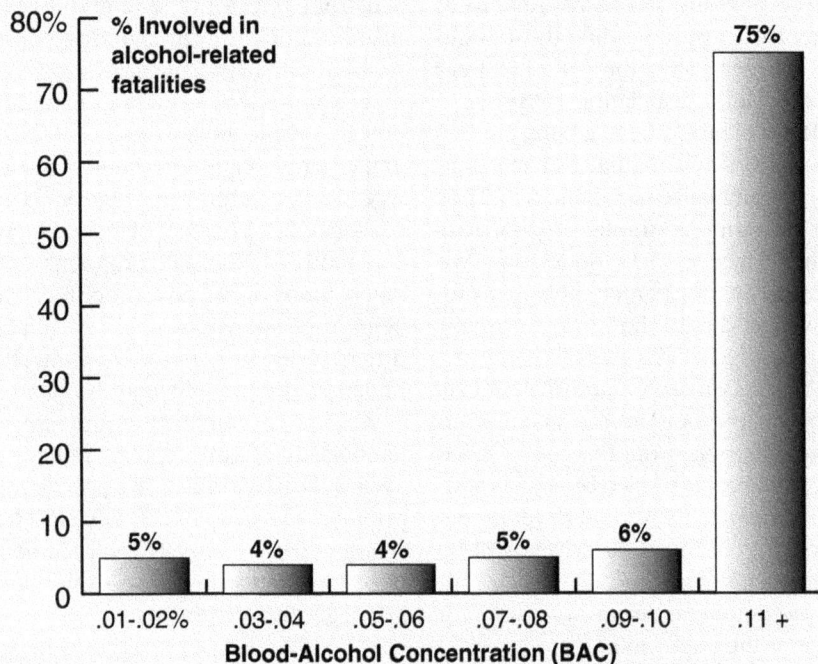

Note: Percentages do not add to 100 due to rounding.

Source: The Century Council, funded by America's leading distillers; National Highway Traffic Safety Administration, Sept. 2, 1999.

above .10 percent, which would make them legally drunk in all 50 states.

"Intoxication is so common among injured drivers, particularly on weekends and holidays, that it is not uncommon for many trauma surgeons and nurses to think that all of their patients are drunk," Soderstrom wrote recently. [6]

But privacy laws prevent ER doctors from proactively notifying police that a driver they are treating appears drunk or tested positive for alcohol. The investigating officer or witnesses must have noticed signs of drunkenness by the driver, and the officer must go to the ER and demand a blood sample that can then be tested at a police lab.

State legislators, ER professionals, police and insurance companies are debating whether ER personnel should be compelled to automatically report drunken drivers to police, just as they have been required to do for decades regarding gunshot victims and those suspected of abuse.

The debate often pits the police — anxious to get a conviction — against medical personnel anxious to protect doctor-patient confidentiality and the sanctity of medical records.

Some hospital administrators also worry that medical insurance companies may start denying reimbursement of expenses for patients who drive drunk. Some trauma centers have recently stopped automatically testing BAC levels out of fear either that they may not be reimbursed or that doctors will be tied up in court.

State legislatures are increasingly debating the issue, and eight states have recently revised their physician-patient privilege laws to either allow or require doctors to report drunken drivers.

Although some ER doctors feel they should be able to call the police to report drunken drivers, the American College of Emergency Physicians and the Emergency Nurses' Association both

ing traffic flow. And once injured drunken drivers enter an ambulance or ER, state privacy laws often protect their medical records.

"It's a huge hole in the system through which large numbers of drunk drivers are not getting detected," says Carol Bononno, an emergency nurse at the Oregon Health Sciences University Hospital.

Intoxicated drivers familiar with drunken-driving laws often escape detection by demanding to be taken to a hospital, even if they only have a scratch, says Carl A. Soderstrom, professor of surgery at the University of Maryland Medical Center in Baltimore.

"They know that once they make it to the ER, they are home free," says Stephen Simon, associate professor of clinical education at the University of Minnesota College of Law.

Yet by some estimates, Soderstrom says, 30 percent to 50 percent of injured drivers were drinking just before arriving at an emergency room, and the overwhelming majority have blood-alcohol levels well support a more limited "responsive re-porting" policy, in which medical personnel can answer a question or provide BAC levels, but only if asked by a law-enforcement officer.

MADD wants medical personnel to report any positive BAC test results in traffic crashes resulting in fatalities or serious injury. The group also calls for immunity from liability for medical personnel providing such information.

Requiring such reporting would provide a more realistic count of actual drunken-driving cases and would enable more victims to be compensated by state victims' compensation funds, MADD says.

Soderstrom, whose trauma center tests the BAC levels of 95 percent of its patients, says such testing is essential for the proper medical and pain management of emergency cases, and to identify chronic alcohol abusers who should be referred for treatment.

But he agrees with NCADD's voluntary policy — at least for now — because of the high percentage of judges who only slap drunken drivers on the wrist. "Before one mandates that doctors and nurses report drunk drivers and spend lots of time involved in court cases, we need higher drunk-driving conviction rates in this country," he says.

The University of Minnesota's Simon argues, however, that testing all injured drivers, regardless of whether they appear to have been drinking, is "an inappropriate use of limited resources."

Should police confiscate the vehicles of drunken drivers?

Since February 1999, New York City has confiscated cars of those arrested for drunken driving, and two Long Island counties (Nassau and Suffolk) have adopted similar policies.

Although police in New York and more than 20 other states were already allowed to confiscate the cars of repeat offenders, Mayor Rudolph

W. Giuliani ordered police to also seize cars of first-time offenders. And just to make sure New Yorkers understood that he was serious, the mayor said the city might pursue permanent confiscation of some cars, even if the drivers were acquitted. By the end of the first year, police had seized 1,458 cars and begun forfeiture actions on 827. [7]

"We wanted to do everything we possibly could to make people think a second, third, fourth or fifth time . . . before getting behind the wheel of a car" and convince them that driving while intoxicated "is a grave, grave error and a crime," he wrote recently. [8]

Further, the mayor said, cracking down on first-time offenders was justified because first-time offenders cause 70 percent of drunken-driving fatalities in the United States.

Giuliani's get-tough policy seems to be working. During the first 11 months of the program, DWI crashes in New York City dropped more than 17 percent, and the number of DWI fatalities declined 18 percent, compared to the same period the previous year, Giuliani points out. "The number of people we've had to arrest for DWI has fallen by 24 percent," he wrote. [9]

MADD strongly supports the program. "These drunken drivers are using their cars as 4,000-pound weapons and are causing a tremendous amount of carnage on our streets and highways," said Maureen Fisher Ricardella, head of the New York City chapter. [10]

But Norman Siegel, executive director of the New York Civil Liberties Union, says the New York law violates the Constitution's innocent-until-proven-guilty clause. Moreover, he says, it severely penalizes innocent drivers who may be deprived of their cars for months while trying to prove their innocence.

Civil libertarians also question the disproportionate punishments resulting from the one-size-fits-all law, under which one motorist might lose a $40,000

car while another might forfeit a car worth only $1,000 for the same offense.

Siegel challenged the law last year, but a state judge ruled on May 19, 1999, that his group had not demonstrated that it was "unconstitutional, contrary to law or arbitrary and capricious." But Siegel vowed to continue the challenge, if necessary all the way to the U.S. Supreme Court. "We continue to believe the initiative is unfair and excessive," he said. [11]

Generally speaking, the Supreme Court has upheld the use of forfeiture by prosecutors, who have used similar statutes to seize the property of drug traffickers. "The idea of going at people through their property has a long history," said Daniel C. Richman, a professor at Fordham Law School. "I think seizing cars on DWI-related theories is state-of-the-art forfeiture law." [12] ■

BACKGROUND

Drunken Charioteers

There have been drunken drivers as long as there have been vehicles. An intoxicated Noah had difficulty maneuvering the ark, and drunken charioteers caused problems in Roman times. [13]

In the 19th century, the problem was intoxicated railroad engineers. In 1843, the New York Central Railroad prohibited employees from drinking while on duty, according to James B. Jacobs, author of *Drunk Driving, an American Dilemma*. [14]

By the turn of the century, after the automobile arrived on the scene, alcohol began playing an unprecedented role in serious and fatal traffic injuries. "Inebriates and moderate drinkers are the most incapable of all persons to drive power motor wagons," said the authors of a 1904 article in the *Quarterly Journal of Inebriety.* [15]

By 1910, states had begun adding drunken-driving offenses to their traffic codes. But federal attention and resources were not mobilized to attack the problem until 1966, when NHTSA's precursor, the National Highway Safety Bureau, was established. A 1968 report by the fledgling agency found that alcohol use by drivers and pedestrians caused 25,000 deaths and 800,000 accidents a year. [16]

First Major Initiative

Two years later, in 1970, NHTSA launched the first major federal initiative against drunken driving — the $88 million Alcohol Safety Action Project — a mix of stepped-up enforcement, rehabilitation and public-information campaigns in 35 cities. DWI arrests in some jurisdictions jumped more than 300 percent, and tens of thousands of drivers received treatment at rehab centers. But the program was not renewed after studies couldn't confirm that it was reducing drunken driving. [17]

By the early 1980s, NHTSA mandated that states enact anti-drunken-driving strategies in order to qualify for federal highway funds. About the same time, two grass-roots victims' organizations cropped up, one on each coast. Remove Intoxicated Drivers (RID) was founded in Schenectady, N.Y., in 1978, and MADD two years later in Sacramento, Calif.

Both groups received federal grants and plenty of press and TV coverage. In 1983 NBC aired a documentary about the life of Candy Lightener, the founder of MADD, whose daughter was killed by a chronic drunken driver. MADD's membership rolls promptly doubled.

In 1982, President Reagan appointed a Presidential Commission on Drunk Driving, which in a 1983 report made more than 50 recommendations, including raising the legal drinking age to 21. In 1984, Congress did just that, passing the Minimum Uniform Drinking Age Act. The law saves about 1,000 lives a year, according to NHTSA.

Since then, pressured by federal legislation linking highway funds to adoption of stricter drunken-driving laws, states have passed a variety of sanctions — including mandatory jail terms, increased fines and automatic and lengthier license suspensions. Others have restricted plea-bargaining or imposed home detention with electronic monitoring.

The policies have paid off. From 1970 to 1986, DWI arrests nationwide increased nearly 223 percent. Between 1982 and 1998, the proportion of traffic deaths involving alcohol dropped 18 percent. [18]

Progress Slows

In 1994, however, the decline in DWI arrests began to slow down, and alcohol-related traffic deaths leveled off. Safety advocates say a variety of trends contributed to the slowdown, including a shift in the national mood — toward more states' rights — following the Republican takeover of Congress. Congress now insists that states be granted greater freedom to decide how to spend federal highway safety dollars.

In addition, safety advocates say, other social issues — such as crime, drugs and violence — have captured the public's attention, while aggressive driving and air bags became the "hot" traffic-safety issues.

Nonetheless, in 1995 NHTSA set the ambitious goal of reducing alcohol-related driving fatalities from the

current level of 15,786 deaths to 11,000 by 2005. But safety advocates fear that will be difficult to attain because the attention of legislators, the public and the media has waned.

Plus, the restaurant and alcohol industries have spread large amounts of money around state capitols and Congress. According to a recent study by Common Cause, alcohol interests gave $22.7 million in campaign contributions to members of Congress and the national political parties in the past 10 years. And, the citizens' lobbying group says, alcohol interests spent another $22 million on salaries and entertainment expenses for lobbyists just between 1997 and the first half of 1999. [19]

In addition, in 1998 restaurant and alcohol-related businesses donated another $12.5 million to governors and state legislators in the 33 states tracked by the National Institute on Money in State Politics. Most of that money went to California, Illinois and Texas. [20]

The growing political strength of the opponents of anti-drunken-driving laws became evident in 1998, when MADD was handed a major political loss. After intense lobbying by alcohol and restaurant groups, Congress adopted a compromise provision that provided incentives — rather than sanctions — for states to move to the stricter .08 BAC standard. Since then, only two states have adopted the tougher standard. [21]

Meanwhile, during the past four years, proposed .08 legislation has been killed in numerous states, leading MADD's Webb to charge that lawmakers have "buckled under pressure from alcohol industry lobbyists."

"In the early days in the fight against drunk driving, MADD, the hospitality industry and law enforcement marched in lock step against drunk driving," Berman says. Since then, he says, advocates of .08 have launched a "holy war" against moderate drinkers, instead of focusing on hard-core alcoholics. "The issue has split our united front." ■

Chronology

CURRENT SITUATION

Action in Congress

The debate over whether states should have to adopt the stricter .08 percent drunken-driving standard was one of several thorny issues that delayed adoption of a $58 billion transportation spending bill. After weeks of bitter lobbying, a compromise .08 provision was adopted by House-Senate conferees on Oct. 3.

The compromise, offered by Senate Majority Whip Don Nickles, R-Okla., would delay implementation of the .08 requirement until 2004. States that don't adopt the stricter standard by then would lose 2 to 8 percent of their highway construction funds each year that they are not in compliance. If a state adopts the .08 standard by fiscal 2007, it would recover the lost funds.

"This is a victory for the American people — a triumph of the public interest over special interests," said Sen. Frank Lautenberg, D-N.J., who had championed the Senate's original version. "Today we put the brakes on drunk driving and saved hundreds of lives by making .08 the standard for every state."

During the fight, money poured in to campaign coffers from the alcohol industry. According to the Center for Responsive Politics, the alcohol industry contributed $6 million in the current election cycle, up one-third from the 1995-96 cycle. Anheuser-Busch Companies Inc. contributed more than $1 million to the total. [22]

NCADD's Moulden attributed Congress' action in part to public outrage over the recent Ford-Firestone tire controversy. "When the American public

1970s-1980s
Drunken-driving victims' groups turn public opinion against drinking and driving. Federal government mandates that states enact anti-drunken-driving strategies to qualify for highway funds.

1970
First major federal initiative against drunken driving — the $88 million Alcohol Safety Action Project — is launched. DWI arrests jump more than 300 percent in some jurisdictions.

1978
Remove Intoxicated Drivers is founded in Schenectady, N.Y.

1980
Mothers Against Drunk Drivers (MADD) is founded in Sacramento, Calif., later changed to Mothers Against Drunk Driving.

1983
Commission on Drunk Driving appointed by President Reagan makes more than 50 recommendations, including raising the legal drinking age to 21. TV movie about MADD boosts group's growth. Utah becomes first state to pass a .08 BAC law.

July 17, 1984
National Minimum Drinking Age Act sets 21 as the minimum drinking age nationwide.

—————— • ——————

1990s-Present
Federal government steps up its campaign against under-age drinking and drunken driving.

1994
DWI arrests slow down, and alcohol-related traffic deaths level off.

January 1995
Administration establishes a goal of reducing alcohol-related driving fatalities to no more than 11,000 by 2005.

July 1995
A provision sponsored by Rep. Scott L. Klug, R-Wis., allowing states to lower their drinking age without losing federal highway funds, is defeated.

May 1996
Legislation authored by Klug to sever the link between a state's drinking age and federal highway funds dies in committee.

1998
Congress offers incentive grants to pressure states to reduce the legal blood-alcohol level from .10 percent to .08 percent. States that don't go along by 2001 would lose federal highway money.

June 15, 2000
Senate adopts measure mandating states to adopt the .08 BAC standard or lose about $1 billion in highway construction funds. MADD celebrates its 20th birthday, with 3 million members and supporters. Alcohol-related fatalities represent 38 percent of total fatalities, down from 55 percent in 1980.

How Hard-Core Drunken Drivers Get Off Easy

The family was driving home in DuPage County, Ill., after a wedding on Aug. 12, when suddenly a white van crashed through their minivan's windshield, remembers 7-year-old Kanwarjot Dhami. He and his sister Prinkia survived, but not their parents and grandparents.

The driver of the white van had a revoked license and a blood-alcohol concentration (BAC) twice the legal limit. In fact, two years earlier, he had been charged with drunken driving on the same road. [1]

In Illinois and around the country, such incidents have led to public demands for a crackdown on hard-core drunken drivers — those who repeatedly drive with BAC levels of .15 percent or above. An average-sized man would need to consume seven drinks in an hour to reach the .15 level.

Hard-core drunken drivers cause much of the slaughter on America's highways, according to a recent National Transportation Safety Board (NTSB) study. In 1998, 17 people were killed *every day* in collisions involving such drivers — at an estimated cost of at least $5.3 billion. [2]

High-BAC drivers make up only 1 percent of all drivers on weekend nights but are involved in nearly half of the fatal crashes during those hours. And 35 percent to 40 percent of drinking drivers killed in traffic collisions had at least one prior driving while intoxicated (DWI) conviction.

But across the country, many state laws and judges repeatedly grant such offenders multiple "second" chances. They do not consider them as felons and often do not require them to serve jail time.

Safety advocates say many judges are reluctant to send drunken drivers to already crowded jails or revoke a driver's license or confiscate a car for fear it will prevent them or other family members from getting to work.

The NTSB and a variety of safety groups recommend a variety of proven-effective measures to get hard-core drunken drivers off the road. For instance, The Century Council, a think tank funded by America's leading distillers, recommends saturation patrols and sobriety checkpoints, statewide DWI reporting systems and increasing the penalties for refusing a breathalyzer or blood-alcohol test. "Without statewide reporting systems, police officers don't know from one county to the next whether someone is a repeat offender," says William P. Georges, the council's vice president for traffic safety.

Among other things, the group also recommends administrative license revocation (ALR) — on-the-spot suspension of suspected drunken drivers' licenses if they fail or refuse a sobriety test. ALR is the "single most effective action a state can take to reduce alcohol-related crashes and fatalities," Georges says. States with ALR laws typically see a 6 percent to 9 percent reduction in alcohol-related traffic fatalities, he says.

Chronic drunken drivers should be forced to undergo alcoholism treatment, Georges says, and there must be intensive supervision after the treatment is finished. Finally, safety advocates recommend graduated penalties, which increase according to the driver's BAC levels and multiplicity of offenses.

The biggest obstacle to such crackdowns, says William Bronrott, a Democratic Maryland legislator, is "the old-boy attitude that, 'There but for the grace of God go I.' "

John Moulden, president of the National Commission Against Drunk Driving, agrees. "The problem isn't a lack of legislation, but the absence of our collective commitment and political will to use the statutes and countermeasures we already have."

Sukhminder Dhami, whose niece and nephew were orphaned in the DuPage County crash, has her own suggestion for getting the repeat drunken driver who killed her family off the road. "He should be hanged," said the immigrant from India. [3]

---

[1] "Man formally charged in traffic collision that killed four people in Hanover Park," *The Associated Press*, Aug. 14, 2000.

[2] "Actions to Reduce Fatalities, Injuries, and Crashes Involving the Hard Core Drinking Driver," National Transportation Safety Board, June 2000.

[3] Jeff Coen and Noreen S. Ahmed Ullah, "Youngsters Awaken to Family's Nightmare; 2 Generations Killed in Crash Tied to DUI, *Chicago Tribune*, Aug. 15, 2000, p. 4.

gets turned on to a highway-safety issue," he says, "the groundswell can swamp any economic interest involved."

The ABI's Berman, who says that "emotion won out over evidence," hasn't given up the fight. "This is still a very contentious issue and a lot of state highway administrators are upset about it. Maybe the four-year delay will allow people more time to reflect on it."

Underage Drinking

The Century Council, a research group funded by distillers, calls youth drinking "one of society's most serious health concerns." [23] Alcohol-related traffic fatalities among drivers under age 21 declined by 60 percent from 1982 to 1998; still, in 1998, 2,730 young drivers were involved in fatal crashes. To combat the problem, the council supports zero-tolerance laws for underage drunken drivers.

The council also supports administrative license revocation (ALR), because 90 percent of teenagers say they would not drink and drive if it meant losing their license. Under ALR, teens caught driving with illegal BACs lose their license on the spot.

Besides pushing for .08 BAC laws, MADD has expanded its mission to stop

Continued on p. 90

At Issue:

Should states lower the BAC arrest threshold for drunken driving to .08 percent?

MILLIE I. WEBB

NATIONAL PRESIDENT, MOTHERS AGAINST DRUNK DRIVING

WRITTEN FOR THE CQ RESEARCHER, OCTOBER 2000

*m*ost Americans support lowering the legal drunken-driving limit to .08 percent blood-alcohol concentration (BAC), according to a new Gallup survey. No reasonable person would want to get on the road or in the car with a .08 percent BAC driver.

Although it's never safe to get behind the wheel after drinking, scientific research shows that virtually everyone is impaired at the .08 level. No matter how many drinks it takes to get to a .08 BAC, driving skills — braking, steering and reaction time — are seriously impaired at that level.

A 170-pound man would have to consume four drinks in an hour on an empty stomach before reaching .08. A 137-pound woman would reach .08 after three drinks. The risk of a fatal crash is at least 11 times greater at .08 BAC.

Opponents argue that .08 doesn't address the real problem. I am living proof that they are wrong. My family was destroyed by a crash caused by a .08 driver, which killed my 4-year-old daughter Lori and baby nephew Mitchell. The crash also caused my husband and me to suffer severe injuries and burns and caused the premature birth and legal blindness of my other daughter, Kara. After two dozen surgeries and two funerals, I can tell you firsthand of the importance of passing .08. One precious life lost is one too many. We can save 500 lives each year if every state passes .08.

Although .08 may seem like common sense to most of us, 31 states still define intoxicated driving as .10 BAC — the most lenient definition of drunken driving in the industrialized world.

The alcohol lobby has worked hard to keep .08 at bay, despite widespread public support. Since 1996, .08 bills have been killed in more than three dozen states as lawmakers buckled under pressure from the alcohol and hospitality industries. The .08 laws aren't getting passed at the state level, and federal incentive grants provide little real incentive.

There is no magic wand to solve the drunken-driving problem. It demands a comprehensive solution with strong law-enforcement efforts, public awareness and effective legislation, including the all-important .08 laws.

Congress has the opportunity to save lives and eliminate "blood borders" between states by passing a federal drunken-driving limit of .08 BAC. Congress and states'-rights supporter Ronald Reagan took the same approach in passing the federal 21 drinking-age law.

There is a time to put the public's interest ahead of the special interests. The time is now.

RICK BERMAN

GENERAL COUNSEL, AMERICAN BEVERAGE INSTITUTE

WRITTEN FOR THE CQ RESEARCHER, OCTOBER 2000

*t*he "one drink equals impairment" crowd is taking us through the looking glass one more time. These anti-alcohol nannies are once again trying to get the federal government to withhold highway money used for building safer roads from states that refuse to arrest moderate drinkers who drive.

Consider the following from Candy Lightner, founder of Mothers Against Drunk Driving: "I worry that the movement I helped create has lost direction. [Focusing on .08 BAC legislation] ignores the real core of the problem."

The General Accounting Office, commenting on the most widely cited study supporting .08, called the three-page study "unfounded." After the California Department of Motor Vehicles and the University of North Carolina studied their own states' .08 laws, both found no effect on drunken driving.

Of course, the National Highway Traffic Safety Administration (NHTSA) and MADD believe otherwise. In 1997, NHTSA Deputy Administrator Phillip Recht told a Senate committee of a study that found 12 percent fewer drunken-driving fatalities resulting from California's .08 law. He didn't mention that the 12 percent figure was only a 1991 prediction. It proved to be false one year later. The real figure, 6.1 percent, actually was slightly worse than the improvement experienced by the rest of the country.

When NHTSA was confronted with its own calculation that under .08 laws, a 120-pound woman would be facing jail after having two 6-ounce glasses of wine over two hours, the agency denied it was possible — until NHTSA's own department head acknowledged it was true.

The Washington Post also has been on an anti-drunken-driving jihad for years. Describing the .08 level of impairment, the *Post* suggests arrest and imprisonment are warranted. However, the *Post* has a different view when it comes to cell phone use, even though *The New England Journal of Medicine* called cell phone users more dangerous than .08 drivers. On this impairment, the *Post* timidly suggests some new restrictions "wouldn't be a bad thing."

The drunken-driving problem of the early 1980s has evolved dramatically. People in control of their drinking behavior obey the new laws. Drunken driving exists today at a new level — what Katherine Prescott, past president of MADD, labeled "a hard core of alcoholics who do not respond to public appeals." Passing new laws aimed at everyone else is truly a Lewis Carroll knockoff.

Continued from p. 88
underage drinking. Young people are involved in more fatal crashes involving alcohol than any other segment of the population, and as the youthful population continues to grow, so does alcohol usage among teenagers. Binge drinking is becoming increasingly popular among high schoolers, MADD says.

OUTLOOK

'Stuck in Neutral'?

Reaching the administration's goal of reducing alcohol-related traffic deaths to 11,000 by 2005 may prove to be a daunting task, safety advocates say. From 1982 to 1999, alcohol-related fatalities dropped an astonishing 37 percent. Reaching the new goal would require an additional 31 percent drop — in half the time.

Complacency may threaten that goal. "When it comes to drunk driving," says the NCADD's Moulden, "our outrage has tempered, and our efforts seem to have run out of steam. Absent the media coverage of earlier years, some people — including state and national legislators — think we have solved this problem."

"We're stuck in neutral on drunken driving," says Jackie Gillan, vice president of Advocates for Highway and Auto Safety, a coalition of insurers, citizens' groups and safety organizations. "We're not making the kind of gains that we should."

Money may also threaten the goal of lowering the death toll, says MADD's Anderson. "The interest groups that oppose stricter state BAC laws are very well-funded and very powerful," she says.

Bronrott, who has followed the issue as both a congressional staffer and now as a Maryland legislator,

agrees. "Believe me, legislator-lobbyist relationships are a lot more chummy in the state capitols than they are in Washington," he says. The alcohol industry in particular "has more leverage at the state level than at the federal level."

Given those ties, he says, "without federal action requiring states to adopt a .08 sanction bill, we will never get all 50 states to adopt a .08 level."

At the moment, industry analysts say, specialty beer and wine sales are up, because of the booming economy and the growth in the 21- to 34-year-old population, which drinks more beer. And as restaurants continue to serve super-size beverages, the amount of alcohol per drink has doubled in some cases.

Nonetheless, over the long term, the ABI's Berman says, "Americans are drinking less alcohol per capita than they did 20 years ago."

Whatever happens with the .08 BAC laws, MADD's Webb says the real long-term problem is getting judges and prosecutors to change the way they treat repeat offenders, as well as first-time drunken drivers.

"With more efforts at educating judges," she says, "we'll eventually have a judicial system that is more accountable."

Carlson, the Illinois housewife hit by a drunken driver, isn't waiting for lawmakers to make changes. For 20 years, she has been telling schoolchildren and police officers — in gruesome detail — how drunken drivers can destroy lives.

"I want to scare the hell out of them" she says. "Kids pass out on me all the time. I even had three state police officers pass out once." ■

Notes

[1] According to National Highway Traffic Safety Administration (NHTSA) figures.

[2] Daniel Hungerford, et al., "Screening for Alcohol Problems May Lessen the Risk," Centers for Disease Control and Prevention, Issue Forum: Drunk Driving, *The Washington Post*, Dec. 13, 1999.

[3] Injury costs include $40 billion in health care, car damages, legal fees and court costs, and $70 billion in lost quality-of-life, according to NHTSA's Web site: www.nhtsa. dot.gov/people/injury/alcohol/scost/us.htm.

[4] Quoted in Jeff Plungis, "Senate Passes Lean Transportation Bill, Expecting It to Bulk Up in Conference," *CQ Weekly*, June 17, 2000.

[5] Stephen Simon, "Medical Staff Reporting of Alcohol Levels Should be Mandatory," Issue Forum: Drunk Driving, *The Washington Post*, Dec. 13, 1999.

[6] Carl A. Soderstrom, "Testing Injured Drivers for Blood Alcohol Content is Valuable," Issue Forum: Drunk Driving, *The Washington Post*, Dec. 13, 1999.

[7] Juan Forero, "Police Ease Car Seizures in Some Drunken Driving Cases," *The New York Times*, January 21, 2000.

[8] Rudolph W. Giuliani, "Policy Makes Progress in the Fight Against Drunk Driving," Issue Forum: Drunk Driving, *The Washington Post*, Dec. 13, 1999.

[9] *Ibid.*

[10] Quoted in Michael Cooper, "Driving Drunk To Mean Loss Of the Vehicle," *The New York Times*, Jan. 22, 1999.

[11] Kit R. Roane, "City Wins Ruling on DWI Crackdown," *The New York Times*, May 20, 1999.

[12] Quoted in Alan Finder, "Drive Drunk, Lose the Car? Principle Faces a Test," *The New York Times*, Feb. 24, 1999.

[13] "Epidemiology of Alcohol-Related Accidents and the Grand Rapids Study," *Forensic Science Review*, Jan. 2000.

[14] James B. Jacobs, *Drunk Driving, an American Dilemma,* University of Chicago Press, 1989, p. xiv.

[15] Quoted in *Forensic Science Review, op cit.*

[16] "Alcohol and Highway Safety," Department of Transportation, 1968.

[17] Jacobs, *op cit.*, p. xv.

[18] *Ibid.*, p. xviii.

[19] "Paying the Price: How Tobacco Gun, Gambling and Alcohol Interests Block Common Sense Solutions to Some of the Nation's Most Urgent Problems," *Common Cause*, June 15, 2000.

[20] According to their Web site, at www.followthemoney.org/database.

[21] For details, see 1998 *CQ Almanac*, p. 24-3.

[22] *Ibid.*

[23] The Century Council, "Looking Back, Moving Forward," March 2000, p. 6.

Bibliography

Selected Sources Used

Books

Jacobs, James B., Drunk Driving, an American Dilemma, *University of Chicago Press,* **1989.**
  Jacobs examines the rise of drunken driving and ways to control it through deterrence, insurance surcharges, tort liability, public education and rehabilitation.

Articles

Finder, Alan, "Drive Drunk, Lose the Car? Principle Faces a Test," *The New York Times,* **Feb. 24, 1999.**
  Finder discusses how the U.S. Supreme Court has generally upheld the use of property forfeiture, such as New York City's new law to confiscate the cars of drunken drivers.

Giuliani, Rudolph W., "Policy Makes Progress in the Fight Against Drunk Driving," *The Washington Post,* **Dec. 13, 1999.**
  The mayor of New York City defends his new policy of confiscating the vehicles of drunken drivers, using the legal principle that private property used in a crime can be confiscated.

Plungis, Jeff, "Transportation Bill Conference Driven by National Drunken Driving Standard, Limitation on Truckers' Road Hours," *CQ Weekly,* **Aug. 5, 2000.**
  Reporter Plungis discusses how the transportation bill conference is deadlocked over the issues of forcing states to adopt a .08 BAC and stopping federal regulators from limiting truck drivers' hours of service.

Simon, Stephen, "Medical Staff Reporting of Alcohol Levels Should be Mandatory," *The Washington Post,* **Dec. 13, 1999.**
  An associate professor of clinical education at the University of Minnesota College of Law argues that emergency medical staff should be required or at least allowed to report drunken drivers who are injured in crashes.

Soderstrom, Carl A., "Testing Injured Drivers for Blood Alcohol Content is Valuable," *The Washington Post,* **Dec. 13, 1999.**
  A professor of surgery at the University of Maryland Medical Center in Baltimore argues that checking the BAC of injured drivers is valuable for medical purposes, but he stops short of recommending that medical personnel should be required to report such information to police.

Studies

"Alcohol and Highway Safety," U.S. Department of Transportation, 1968.
  The first federal study on alcohol consumption and driver impairment found that alcohol use by drivers and pedestrians caused 25,000 deaths and 800,000 accidents.

"Paying the Price: How Tobacco, Gun, Gambling and Alcohol Interests Block Common Sense Solutions to Some of the Nation's Most Urgent Problems," Common Cause, June 15, 2000.
  A study of campaign contributions shows that alcohol interests gave $22.7 million in campaign contributions to members of Congress and the national political parties from 1989 to 1999.

Stewart, Kathryn, "On DWI Laws in Other Countries," National Highway Traffic Safety Administration, March 2000.
  A comprehensive study compares laws governing drunken driving in 22 countries.

Highway Safety:
Effectiveness of State .08 Blood Alcohol Laws

GAO
United States
General Accounting Office
Washington, D.C. 20548
Resources, Community, and
Economic Development Division

B-280883

June 23, 1999

The Honorable John McCain
Chairman
The Honorable Ernest F. Hollings
Ranking Minority Member
Committee on Commerce, Science, and
    Transportation
United States Senate

The Honorable Bud Shuster
Chairman
The Honorable James L. Oberstar
Ranking Democratic Member
Committee on Transportation and
    Infrastructure
House of Representatives

In 1997, someone in the United States died in an alcohol-related motor vehicle crash every 32 minutes. For years, the Congress and the states have grappled with and sought solutions to the problem of drunk driving. Most states have laws making it illegal for people to drive with a specified level of alcohol in their blood, usually set at .10 blood alcohol concentration (BAC)—the level at which a person's blood contains 1/10th of 1 percent alcohol. However, 16 states have more stringent laws setting the limit at .08 BAC. In 1998, the Clinton administration endorsed a bill that would have required all states to enact and enforce .08 BAC laws or face reductions in federal highway funds. The Senate approved this bill; the House took no action.

The Transportation Equity Act for the 21st Century directed GAO to evaluate the effectiveness of state .08 BAC laws in reducing the number and severity of crashes involving alcohol.[1] To accomplish this objective, we reviewed (1) the policies and positions of the Department of Transportation's (DOT) National Highway Traffic Safety Administration (NHTSA) on .08 BAC laws and other drunk driving countermeasures and (2) seven published studies on the effect of .08 BAC laws on the number and severity of crashes involving alcohol, including three studies released on April 28, 1999.

Results in Brief

Overall, the evidence does not conclusively establish that .08 BAC laws, by themselves, result in reductions in the number and severity of alcohol-related crashes. There are, however, strong indications

---

[1]The Transportation Equity Act for the 21st Century also directed us to study the effectiveness of .02 BAC laws for drivers under 21 in reducing the number and severity of crashes involving alcohol. The National Highway System Designation Act of 1995 required all states to enact and enforce such laws or face reductions in federal highway funds. However, as agreed to by your staff, we will not address the impact of .02 BAC laws, since all 50 states and the District of Columbia now have laws establishing BAC levels of .02 or less for drivers under 21.

that .08 BAC laws in combination with other drunk driving laws (particularly license revocation laws), sustained public education and information efforts, and vigorous and consistent enforcement can save lives. For example, while two studies have concluded that California's .08 BAC law was not directly associated with the decline in drunk driving deaths the state experienced in the early 1990s, these studies found that the .08 BAC law was effective when paired with the state's license revocation law, which took effect 6 months later.

Until recently, only four published studies examined the effectiveness of .08 BAC laws in five states and, while NHTSA characterized the studies as conclusively establishing that .08 BAC laws by themselves were effective, the studies had limitations and raised methodological concerns calling their conclusions into question or reported mixed results. In April 1999, three additional studies were released that were more comprehensive and showed many positive results but nevertheless fell short of providing conclusive evidence that .08 BAC laws were, by themselves, responsible for reductions in alcohol-related crashes and fatalities. It is difficult to accurately predict how many lives would be saved if all states enacted .08 BAC laws because whether a state sees reductions after enacting a .08 BAC law depends on a number of factors, including the degree to which the law is publicized, how well it is enforced, other drunk driving laws in effect, and public attitudes concerning alcohol. Despite the absence of a strong causal link between .08 BAC laws by themselves and reductions in traffic fatalities, other evidence, including medical evidence on drivers' impairment, should be considered when evaluating the effectiveness of .08 BAC laws.[2]

Background

It is illegal in every state and the District of Columbia to drive a motor vehicle while under the influence of alcohol. In addition, all states but two have blood alcohol "per se" laws—laws that make it unlawful for a person to drive a motor vehicle with a *specific* amount of alcohol in his or her blood. . . . [Thirty-two] states and the District of Columbia have set that amount at .10 BAC. In 16 states, the per se limit is 20 percent lower, or .08 BAC.

On average, according to NHTSA, a 170-pound man reaches .08 BAC after consuming five 12-ounce beers (4.5-percent alcohol by volume) over a 2-hour period. A 120-pound woman reaches the same level after consuming three beers over the same period. NHTSA publishes a BAC estimator that computes the level of alcohol in a person's blood on the basis of the person's weight and gender and the amount of alcohol consumed over a specific period of time. This estimator assumes average physical attributes in the population—in reality, alcohol affects individuals differently, and this guide cannot precisely predict its effect on everyone. For example, younger people have higher concentrations of body water than older people; therefore, after consuming the same amount of alcohol, a 170-pound 20-year-old man attains a lower BAC level on average than a 170-pound 50-year-old man.

. . . NHTSA's estimator shows that the difference between the .08 BAC and .10 BAC levels for a 170-pound man is one beer over 2 hours. The difference between the .08 BAC and .10 BAC levels for a 120-pound woman is one-half a beer over the same time period.

Alcohol use is a significant factor in fatal motor vehicle crashes. In 1997, the most recent year for which data are available, there were 16,189 alcohol-related fatalities, representing 38.6 percent of the nearly 42,000 people killed in fatal crashes that year. In the states with .08 BAC laws, alcohol was involved in 36 percent of all traffic fatalities, lower than the national average and the 39.5-percent rate

---

[2]Because the Transportation Equity Act for the 21st Century directed us to review the effectiveness of .08 BAC laws in reducing the number and severity of crashes involving alcohol, we did not evaluate the medical impairment evidence.

continues

of alcohol involvement in the rest of the states.[3] Utah had the lowest level at 20.6 percent; the District of Columbia had the highest at 58.5 percent. Among the 10 states with the lowest levels of alcohol-related fatalities, 3 were states with .08 BAC laws and 7 were states with .10 BAC laws. Among the 10 states with the highest levels of alcohol-related fatalities, 2 were states with .08 BAC laws, 7 were states with .10 BAC laws, and 1 had no BAC per se law.

Although alcohol use remains a significant factor in fatal crashes, fatalities involving alcohol have declined sharply over the last 15 years. In 1982, 25,165 people died in crashes involving alcohol, 57.3 percent of the nearly 44,000 traffic fatalities that year. The proportion of fatal crashes that involved alcohol declined during the 1980s, falling below 50 percent for the first time in 1989. The involvement of alcohol in fatal crashes declined markedly in the early 1990s, from about 50 percent of the fatal crashes in 1990 to nearly 40 percent in 1994. During this time, the number of people killed in crashes involving alcohol declined by around 25 percent. The proportion of fatalities involving alcohol rose slightly in the next 2 years before falling, in 1997, to its lowest level since 1982. . . .

Each state reports, and NHTSA collects and publishes, data on fatal crashes through the Fatal Accident Reporting System (FARS), a comprehensive national database of all crashes in which a person dies within 30 days of the crash. These data include (1) the number of fatalities that occur in all crashes and (2) the number of drivers involved in fatal crashes. FARS also includes whether crashes involved drivers who had been drinking. However, FARS has limitations regarding alcohol involvement in crashes—for example, fewer than half of the drivers at the scene of fatal accidents are tested for alcohol. To address the missing data, NHTSA developed a statistical model, first used in 1982, to estimate alcohol involvement in cases in which data are not available. The model provides estimates in three broad categories—sober (.00 BAC), "low BAC" (.01–.09 BAC), and "high BAC" (.10 BAC and above).[4] Therefore, certain questions—such as how many fatal crashes involve drivers with .08 BAC levels versus other levels or what the average BAC of drunk drivers involved in fatal crashes is—cannot be reliably answered by this model. NHTSA plans to release a new model in 1999 that will estimate specific BAC levels.

NHTSA Believes All States Should Have Alcohol Deterrence Measures, Including .08 BAC Laws

NHTSA believes that the best countermeasure against drunk driving is a combination of laws, public education, and enforcement. Since 1970, NHTSA has espoused a "systems approach" to reducing drunk driving including enforcement, judicial, legislative, licensing, and public information components. In 1997, NHTSA published an action plan developed with other participants to reduce alcohol-related driving fatalities to 11,000 by the year 2005. This plan recommended that all states pass a wide range of laws, including ones establishing .08 BAC limits, license revocation laws—under which a person deemed to be driving under the influence has his or her driving privileges suspended or revoked—comprehensive screening and treatment programs for alcohol offenders, vehicle impoundment, "zero tolerance" BAC and other laws for youth, and primary enforcement laws for safety belts.[5] The plan also called for increased public awareness campaigns, with an emphasis on target populations such as

---

[3]This analysis excludes Idaho and Illinois, states that had .08 BAC laws take effect during 1997.

[4]When cataloguing fatalities in crashes in which more than one driver had been drinking, FARS uses the driver with the higher BAC.

[5]Primary enforcement laws permit officials to enforce safety belt requirements independently of other traffic safety laws, in contrast to secondary enforcement laws, which allow officials to enforce safety belt requirements only when other traffic safety laws are being enforced.

young people and repeat offenders. Similarly, "The Presidential Initiative for Making .08 BAC the National Legal Limit," published by NHTSA in August 1998, contained a four-point plan that recommended the expansion of public education campaigns; the building of public-private partnerships; and active, high-visibility enforcement of several alcohol laws.

The value of public education and enforcement has been demonstrated in a number of studies. A recent NHTSA evaluation of a sobriety checkpoint program in Tennessee, a state with a .10 BAC limit, concluded that the program and its attendant publicity reduced alcohol-related fatal accidents in the state by 20.4 percent. A systems approach to traffic safety is not limited to preventing drunk driving. Our January 1996 report concluded that the states that have been most successful at increasing safety belt use among all drivers are the ones with primary enforcement laws, visible and aggressive enforcement, and active public information and education programs.[6]

Since 1992, when it first recommended in a report to the Congress that all states have .08 BAC laws, NHTSA's position has changed from urging the states to pass .08 BAC laws to favoring that states be required to do so. The latter position was embodied in the President's endorsement of a Senate bill entitled the Safe and Sober Streets Act. This bill would have required all states to enact and enforce .08 BAC laws by October 1, 2001, or lose 5 percent of certain federal highway funds the first year and 10 percent each succeeding year. The Senate approved this bill on March 4, 1998, but the House took no action before the 105th Congress adjourned.[7]

. . . NHTSA has a number of reasons why it believes all states should adopt .08 BAC laws.

One of NHTSA's principal arguments for nationwide adoption of .08 BAC laws is that the medical evidence of drivers' impairment at that level is substantial and conclusive. According to NHTSA . . . reaction time, tracking and steering, and emergency responses are impaired at even low levels, and ubstantially impaired at .08 BAC. As a result, the risk of being in a motor vehicle crash increases when alcohol is involved, and increases dramatically at .08 BAC and higher levels. In contrast to NHTSA's position, industry associations critical of .08 BAC laws contend that .08 BAC is an acceptable level of impairment for driving a motor vehicle and that these laws penalize "responsible social drinking." These associations also believe that .08 BAC laws do not address the problem of drunk driving because many more drivers using alcohol are reported at the "high" BAC levels (above .10 BAC) than the lower BAC levels.

Because we were directed to review the impact of .08 BAC laws on the number and severity of crashes involving alcohol, we did not review the medical evidence on impairment or other arguments in favor of or in opposition to .08 BAC laws.

NHTSA also believes that lowering the BAC limit to .08 is a proven effective measure that will reduce the number of crashes and save lives. For example, in a December 1997 publication, NHTSA stated that "recent research . . . has been quite conclusive in showing the impaired driving reductions *already attributable to .08*, as well as the potential for saving additional lives if all states adopted .08 BAC laws" (emphasis added). In May 1998, the NHTSA Administrator stated, "The traffic safety administration is aware of four published studies, . . . [and] each study has shown that lowering the illegal blood alcohol limit to .08 is associated with significant reductions in alcohol-related fatal crashes." In a fact sheet distributed to state

---

[6]Motor Vehicle Safety: Comprehensive State Programs Offer Best Opportunity for Increasing Use of Safety Belts (GAO/RCED 96-24, Jan. 3, 1996).

[7]The Senate approved this bill as an amendment to its surface transportation reauthorization bill. However, these provisions were not included in the House bill and were not included in the final version of the Transportation Equity Act for the 21st Century.

continues

legislatures considering these laws, NHTSA stated that the agency's "analysis of five states that lowered the BAC limit to .08 showed that significant decreases in alcohol-related fatal crashes occurred in four out of the five states *as a result of the legislation*" (emphasis added). NHTSA used these study results to encourage states to enact .08 BAC laws, testifying in one instance before a state legislature, "We conservatively project a 10-percent reduction in alcohol-related crashes, deaths, and injuries" in the state.

Seven Studies Have Examined the Effectiveness of .08 BAC Laws.

Seven studies have been published assessing the effect of .08 BAC laws on motor vehicle crashes and fatalities in the United States. Four studies published between 1991 and 1996 assessed the effectiveness of .08 BAC laws in the five states that enacted them between 1983 and 1991. On April 28, 1999, NHTSA released three additional studies. Table 1 summarizes the seven studies that examine .08 BAC laws.

The First Four Published Studies Had Limitations and Raised Methodological Concerns

Although NHTSA characterized the first four studies on the effectiveness of .08 BAC laws as conclusively establishing that .08 BAC laws resulted in substantial reductions in fatalities involving alcohol, we found that three of the four studies had limitations and raised methodological concerns that called their conclusions into question. For example, while a NHTSA-endorsed Boston University study concluded that 500 to 600 fewer fatal crashes would occur each year if all states adopted .08 BAC laws, this study has been criticized for, among other reasons, its method of comparing states; and a recent NHTSA study characterized the earlier study's conclusion as "unwarranted." The fourth study reported mixed results. Therefore, these studies did not provide conclusive evidence that .08 BAC laws by themselves have resulted in reductions in drunk driving crashes and fatalities. A task force of the New Jersey State Senate examined this evidence and, in a report issued in December 1998, reached a similar conclusion.[8]

The California Studies

NHTSA has cited California's experience as evidence of the effectiveness of .08 BAC laws. For example, in a publication promoting the need for .08 BAC laws, NHTSA stated that "alcohol-related fatalities significantly decreased after the state's BAC limit was lowered to .08 in 1990." In another publication, it said "California's .08 law was analyzed by NHTSA, [and] . . . the state experienced a 12% reduction in alcohol-related fatalities, although some of this can be credited to the new administrative license revocation law."

While NHTSA's 1991 study by Research and Evaluation Associates (see table 1) did find a 12-percent decline in alcohol-related fatalities after the .08 BAC law took effect, the study had important limitations. For example, the authors had available to them only 1 year of data for the period after the law went into effect, an unusually short period of time to analyze trends, and the authors acknowledged this lim-

---

[8]State of New Jersey, <u>Senate Task Force on Alcohol-Related Motor Vehicle Accidents and Fatalities</u>, Dec. 11, 1998. Created by the leaders of the New Jersey State Senate, the task force was composed of elected officials and representatives from the state's judicial, medical, academic, and law enforcement communities. The task force was charged with, among other things, evaluating the available studies, and determining whether reducing the BAC limit to .08 would reduce the number of alcohol-related accidents and fatalities in New Jersey. The task force concluded that "the impact of laws that reduce the per se BAC level from .10 to .08 in isolation, is inconclusive" and that the effect of public education and awareness campaigns and license revocation laws "can be greater than changing the legal BAC."

Table 1: Studies on the Effectiveness of .08 BAC Laws

Title to study	Released	Conducted by	Funded by	Scope
The Effects Following the Implementation of an .08 BAC Limit and an Administrative Per Se Law in California	1991	Research and Evaluation Associates	NHTSA	California
A Preliminary Assessment of the Impact of Lowering the Illegal BAC Per Se Limit to .08 in Five States	1994	NHTSA staff	NHTSA	California, Utah, Oregon, Maine, and Vermont
The General Deterrent Impact of California's .08% Blood Alcohol Concentration Limit and Administrative Per Se License Suspension Laws	1995	Department of Motor Vehicles, State of California	California Office of Traffic Safety	California
Lowering State Legal Blood Alcohol Concentration Limits to .08%: The Effect on Fatal Motor Vehicle Crashes	1996	Researchers from Boston University's School of Public Health	Grants, including ones from the National Institute on Alcohol Abuse and Alcoholism and the U.S. Centers for Disease Control and Prevention	California, Utah, Oregon, Maine, and Vermont
The Effects of 0.08 Laws	1999	Rainbow Technology Inc., and NHTSA's National Center for Statistics and Analysis	NHTSA	California, Utah, Oregon, Maine, Vermont, New Hampshire, North Carolina, Kansas, New Mexico, Florida, and Virginia
Evaluation of the Effects of North Carolina's 0.08% BAC Law	1999	University of North Carolina	NHTSA	North Carolina
The Relationship of Alcohol Safety Laws to Drinking Drivers in Fatal Crashes	1999	Pacific Institute for Research and Evaluation	NHTSA	50 states and the District of Columbia

itation. California also had a license revocation law—under which a person deemed to be driving under the influence has his or her driving privileges suspended or revoked—take effect 6 months after the .08 BAC law. Although the authors concluded that this law had no effect, they stated that they were unable to accurately account for the separate effects of the two laws.

A more comprehensive, methodologically sound study of California was released by the state's Department of Motor Vehicles in 1995. In contrast to the 1991 review, this study was based on 4 years of data after the law became effective and found mixed results. The study concluded that the .08 BAC law was not associated with any statistically significant reductions in crashes resulting in fatalities or se-

continues

rious injuries in which drivers were reported to have been drinking, but that reductions did occur in accidents that took place during hours in which alcohol involvement is probable, such as nighttime crashes between 2 and 3 a.m. The study found reductions associated with the state's license revocation law—a 9 to 13 percent decline in crashes resulting in fatalities or serious injuries in which drivers were reported to have been drinking. However, given the 6-month time period separating the effective dates of the two laws, the authors concluded that .08 BAC and license revocation laws most likely worked together to lower fatalities.

Although the 1995 study was more comprehensive than the 1991 study, NHTSA's public statements and literature often quote the 12-percent reduction cited in the 1991 study and rarely refer to the 1995 study. California continued to experience a decline in alcohol-related fatalities through the 1990s—from 47 percent of fatalities in 1991 to 36 percent in 1997. California traffic safety and law enforcement officials believe that this progress is attributable to the combination of stronger laws, a sustained public information campaign, and vigorous enforcement.

The Boston University Study

A 1996 study by researchers from the Boston University School of Public Health published in the American Journal of Public Health compared the first five states to adopt .08 BAC laws with five "nearby" states that retained .10 BAC laws. It found a 16 percent greater decline in the proportion of alcohol-related fatalities among drivers in the states adopting the lower limit and concluded that if all states adopted .08 BAC laws, 500 to 600 fewer fatal crashes would occur annually. These study results were endorsed by NHTSA and often cited in the agency's literature and public statements. President Clinton cited the study in a March 1998 statement and said " . . . if all states lower their BAC to .08, it will result in 600 fewer alcohol-related deaths each year."

However, this study has been criticized by many traffic safety experts both inside and outside of NHTSA and has methodological limitations that call its results into question. For example:

- Many traffic safety experts question this study's method of comparing one state to another. The study does not explain the criteria used to select the comparison states. Using one state as a control to assess the impact of a new law in another state assumes that all other conditions are held equal except for the introduction of the law. One critic noted, for example, that one of the states with a .08 BAC law employs random roadside sobriety checkpoints and was compared to a state with a .10 BAC law that prohibits the practice. Changing the selection of comparison states can dramatically change this study's results. According to NHTSA, while other traffic safety studies have made single state comparisons, it is best to compare one state to several or to the rest of the nation.

- Three of the five states had license revocation laws take effect within 10 months of their .08 BAC laws. This study made no effort to separately analyze the relative contribution of the two types of laws to any subsequent decline in fatal motor vehicle crashes in those three states. Thus, in at least three states, the authors' findings could as easily apply to the license revocation law as the .08 BAC law. The authors acknowledged this limitation, but it is rarely cited in NHTSA's literature and public statements endorsing this study and its findings.

- The study's conclusion that 500 to 600 fewer fatal crashes would occur annually if all states had .08 BAC laws is unfounded. The study does not explain how this estimate was derived or how the reduction could be credited to .08 BAC laws since the .08 BAC and license revocation laws went into effect within 10 months of each other in three of the five states. The authors told us that the estimate assumed that all states without .08 BAC laws would experience a reduction of up to 10 percent in alcohol-related crashes after enacting the laws. However, the study provides no basis for assuming that reductions of that magnitude would occur. Even this particular study found that while three of the five states experienced reductions greater than their comparison state, two of the five did not. NHTSA's April 1999 study of the effect of .08 BAC laws in 11 states (see table 1) characterized this conclusion as "unwarranted."

NHTSA Staff Study

In 1994, NHTSA staff conducted a study that examined FARS data in the first five states that enacted .08 BAC laws (see table 1). NHTSA has often cited this study as evidence of the effectiveness of .08 BAC laws. For example, a December 1997 publication with the National Safety Council said, ". . . significant reductions in alcohol-related fatal crashes were found in 4 out of the 5 states ranging from 4% to 40%. . . ."

The staff study examined 6 measures of alcohol involvement, ranging from fatal crashes involving drivers with high BACs to single-vehicle crashes late at night, in each of the five states (for a total of 30 measures) and found statistically significant decreases in 9 of the 30 measures. The study also had several important limitations, which the authors acknowledged. For example, as with the Boston University study, the staff study made no effort to separately account for the relative contributions of .08 BAC laws and license revocation laws in the three states that enacted them within a short period. The staff study cautioned that the results were preliminary and that they pointed to the need for further research. NHTSA's public statements, however, were more definitive—conveying, for example, the impression that fatal crashes involving alcohol went down 40 percent in one of the five states. However, the 40-percent figure refers to only one of the six measures in Vermont, a state that experiences fairly significant year-to-year variations in fatal crashes. One of the authors told us he viewed the results as indicative of positive but not clear results.

Recent Studies Are More Comprehensive, but Results Are Mixed

On April 28, 1999, NHTSA released three studies that it sponsored (see table 1). These studies are more comprehensive than the earlier studies and show many positive results but fall short of conclusively establishing that .08 BAC laws by themselves have resulted in reductions in alcohol related fatalities. For example, during the early 1990s, when the involvement of alcohol in traffic fatalities declined from around 50 percent to nearly 40 percent—a trend in states with both .08 BAC and .10 BAC laws— eight states' .08 BAC laws became effective, and the recent studies disagree on the degree to which .08 BAC laws played a role. Two of the studies reached different conclusions about the effect of one state's .08 BAC law—one concluded that the law brought about reductions in drunk driving deaths in North Carolina, while another concluded that the state's reductions occurred as the result of a long-term trend that began before the law was enacted. In a statement releasing the three studies, NHTSA credited the nation's progress in reducing drunk driving to a combination of strict state laws and tougher enforcement and stated that "these three studies provide additional support for the premise that .08 BAC laws help to reduce alcohol-related fatalities, particularly when they are implemented in conjunction with other impaired driving laws and programs."

Eleven-State Study

An April 1999 NHTSA study of 11 states with .08 BAC laws (see table 1) assessed whether the states experienced statistically significant reductions in three measures of alcohol involvement in crashes

continues

after the law took effect: (1) the number of fatalities in crashes in which any alcohol was involved, (2) the number of fatalities in crashes where drivers had a BAC of .10 or greater ("high BAC"), and (3) the proportion of fatalities involving "high BAC" drivers to fatalities involving sober drivers. The study performed a similar analysis for license revocation laws and also modeled and controlled for any pre-existing long-term declining trends these states may have been experiencing when their .08 BAC laws went into effect. The study found that 5 of the 11 states had reductions in at least one measure and that 2 of the 11 states had reductions in all three measures. Table 2 summarizes the states and measures for which the study found statistically significant reductions after .08 BAC laws became effective.

Reductions in all three measures of fatalities involving alcohol occurred in Florida and Vermont. Although alcohol involvement in fatal crashes began to decline in Florida before the .08 BAC law was enacted, it continued to do so after the law went into effect on January 1, 1994. According to FARS, the number of alcohol-related traffic deaths in Florida declined in 1994 by nearly 10 percent, while the proportion of fatalities involving alcohol fell from 44 to 39 percent—in 1997 it stood at around 34 percent. While the study noted that Vermont has experienced fluctuations in fatal crash rates, it found that after Vermont's .08 BAC law took effect, it also experienced statistically significant reductions in both the number of fatalities involving alcohol and the proportion of fatalities involving drivers with high BACs to those involving sober drivers. In this study, Vermont was the only state of the first five states to enact .08 BAC laws that showed any reductions in alcohol-related fatalities associated with .08 BAC laws.

Three other states that enacted .08 BAC laws in 1993 and 1994—North Carolina, New Mexico, and Kansas—experienced statistically significant reductions in the proportion of fatalities involving drivers with high BACs to those involving sober drivers. According to one of the authors, this proportion is the most accurate indicator of the study's three measures—the study noted that if fatalities involving sober drivers decline along with alcohol-related fatalities, then some broader cause other than alcohol legislation is affecting all traffic fatalities. However, if the .08 BAC law operates as expected, al-

Table 2: Results of the 11-State Study of .08 BAC Laws

State	Year .08 BAC law became effective	Statistically significant reduction occurred in		
		Alcohol-related fatalities	Fatalities involving "high BAC" drivers	Proportion of fatalities involving "high BAC" drivers to those involving sober drivers
Utah	1983	No	No	No
Oregon	1983	No	No	No
Maine	1988	No	No	No
California	1990	No	No	No
Vermont	1991	**Yes**	**Yes**	**Yes**
Kansas	1993	No	No	**Yes**
North Carolina	1993	No	No	**Yes**
Florida	1994	**Yes**	**Yes**	**Yes**
New Hampshire	1994	No	No	No
New Mexico	1994	No	No	**Yes**
Virginia	1994	No	No	No
Total		2 of 11	2 of 11	5 of 11

Note: "Yes" indicates a statistically significant reduction after the .08 BAC law became effective.
"No" indicates no statistically significant reduction.

cohol-related deaths will decline while deaths involving sober drivers remain unaffected. In Kansas, the proportion of alcohol involvement declined because fatalities involving sober drivers increased while alcohol-related fatalities remained relatively stable, and in North Carolina, fatalities involving sober drivers increased markedly while fatalities involving drivers with high and low BACs continued their preexisting downward trend. The author stated that without the .08 BAC legislation, alcohol-related fatalities would have been expected to increase along with fatalities involving sober drivers.

In two states where no statistically significant reductions occurred after .08 BAC laws became effective in any category—California and Virginia—the study found that the .08 BAC laws were effective when paired with the states' license revocation laws. In both cases, the license revocation laws went into effect after the .08 BAC laws, and the study found that the reductions did not begin until the license revocation laws were in force.

Finally, the study found no statistically significant reductions in four states. Utah experienced no noticeable change in fatalities involving alcohol after enacting both its .08 BAC and license revocation laws in 1983. The authors noted that the rate of alcohol involvement in fatal crashes in Utah was substantially lower than the national average and that further reductions would have been difficult. Fatalities involving alcohol in Oregon showed little change after the .08 BAC law went into effect in 1983—the most dramatic change occurred over 6 years after the law's implementation. Maine experienced no significant reductions in alcohol-related fatalities after its .08 BAC law was implemented in 1988. New Hampshire experienced a decline in alcohol-related fatalities 2 years before its .08 BAC law went into effect in 1993 but saw no significant decline in fatalities associated with the .08 BAC law.

The study was careful to not draw a causal relationship between the reductions it found and the passage of .08 BAC laws by themselves. Rather, it concluded that .08 BAC laws added to the impact that enforcement; public information; and legislative activities, particularly license revocation laws, were having. In addition to the two states where .08 BAC and license revocation laws were found to be effective in combination, the study noted that the five states with .08 BAC laws that showed reductions already had license revocation laws in place. One of the authors told us that this suggested that the .08 BAC laws had the effect of expanding the scope of the license revocation laws to a new portion of the driving public.

University of North Carolina Study

A NHTSA-sponsored study by the University of North Carolina concluded, in contrast to the 11-state study, that the .08 BAC law in North Carolina had little clear effect. The study examined alcohol-related crashes and crashes involving drivers with BACs greater than .10 from 1991 through 1995; compared fatalities among drivers with BACs greater than .10 in North Carolina with such fatalities in 11 other states; and compared six measures of alcohol involvement in North Carolina and 37 states that did not have .08 BAC laws at that time. The study controlled for and commented on external factors that could confound the results, such as the state's sobriety checkpoints, enforcement, and media coverage. The study found the following:

- No statistically significant decrease in alcohol-related crashes after passage of North Carolina's .08 BAC law in three direct and two "proxy" measures.[9]

---

[9]Direct measures are actual observations, such as police reports of alcohol involvement in crashes, whereas proxy measures are not actual observations, but categories in which the involvement of alcohol is considered probable, such as nighttime crashes between 2 and 3 a.m.

continues

- A continual decline in the proportion of fatally injured drivers with BACs equal to or greater than .10 but no abrupt change in fatalities that could be attributed to the .08 BAC law.
- Decreases in alcohol-related crashes in North Carolina and in the 11 other states studied. While North Carolina's decreases were greater, the study concluded that no specific effects could be attributed to the .08 BAC law.
- No statistically significant difference between North Carolina and 37 states without .08 BAC laws in four of the six measures. While reductions in police-reported and estimated instances of alcohol involvement were found to be statistically significant, these reductions happened 18 months before North Carolina lowered its BAC limit. The authors attributed these decreases, in part, to increased enforcement.

The study concluded that the .08 BAC law had little clear effect on alcohol-related fatalities in North Carolina, and that a downward trend was already occurring before North Carolina enacted its .08 BAC law and that this trend was not affected by the law. The author offered several possible explanations, including that (1) the effects of the .08 BAC laws were obscured by a broader change in drinking-driving behavior that was already occurring; (2) North Carolina had made substantial progress combating drunk driving and that the remaining drinking and driving population in North Carolina was simply not responsive to the lower BAC law; and (3) .08 BAC laws are not effective in measurably affecting the behavior of drinking drivers.

50-State Study

The third April 1999 NHTSA study did a complex regression analysis assessing the effect of three drunk driving laws, including .08 BAC laws.[10] It evaluated .08 BAC laws by comparing two groups—states with .08 BAC laws with states with .10 BAC laws, before and after the laws were passed. The study examined quarterly FARS data for all 50 states and Washington, D.C. from 1982 through 1997 and tested for reductions in the involvement of (1) "low BAC" drivers (.01 BAC through .09 BAC) and (2) "high BAC" drivers (.10 BAC and above) in fatal crashes. The study was more comprehensive than the prior multistate studies, having controlled for the effects of factors such as the number of licensed drivers, vehicle miles traveled, per capita beer consumption, unemployment rates, urban/rural composition, season, safety belt laws, and existing downward trends in alcohol-related fatal crashes. This study concluded that states that enacted .08 BAC laws experienced an 8-percent reduction in the involvement of drivers with both high and low BACs when compared with the involvement of sober drivers. The study estimated that 274 lives have been saved in the states that enacted .08 BAC laws and that 590 lives could be saved annually if all states enacted .08 BAC laws.

While more comprehensive than other studies, the study used a method to calculate the 8-percent reduction that is different, and thus not directly comparable, to those for fatality estimates reported in other studies and publications. In particular, this method can produce a numerical effect that is larger than other methods. In the past, NHTSA's statistics and other studies measured differences either (1) in the number of alcohol-related fatalities or the number of drivers reported to have been using alcohol (termed "alcohol-involved" drivers) or (2) in the proportion of such fatalities or drivers as a percentage of all fatalities or drivers. The 50-state study's 8-percent estimate is the change in the ratio of

---

[10]Regression analysis is a statistical technique used to describe and analyze relationships between a dependent variable (e.g. fatal crashes involving alcohol) and one or more independent variables (e.g. .08 BAC and license revocation laws).

alcohol-involved drivers to sober drivers who are in fatal crashes. While this is not an inappropriate way to measure differences in crashes and fatalities, this method can increase the size of the effect because, rather than comparing fatalities or drivers involving alcohol to all fatalities or drivers, it compares the number of alcohol-involved drivers to just the number of sober drivers. This method produced a larger effect in this study because, since 1982, of the drivers involved in fatal crashes, the number reported to have been using alcohol has dramatically declined (by around 39 percent), while the number reported to have been sober has substantially increased (by around 25 percent). While the 11-state study also measured this ratio, that study did not report a numerical effect.

Table 3 illustrates the difference between these methods of portraying traffic statistics using NHTSA's FARS data on drivers involved in fatal crashes between 1995 and 1997. As the table shows, while the number of alcohol-involved drivers declined by about 6 percent, the ratio of such drivers to sober drivers declined by 9 percent.

Another reason why this study's results cannot be directly compared to other studies' is because it did not include data for drivers under 21. In 1997, drivers under 21 accounted for around 14 percent of the drivers in fatal crashes and about 12 percent of the drivers in fatal crashes involving alcohol. According to the authors, drivers under 21 were excluded from the analysis because other laws affect these drivers, such as minimum drinking age and "zero tolerance" BAC laws, and thus the primary effect of .08 BAC legislation would be expected to be on the population over 21 years old. While this argument may have merit, other arguments exist for including this population. First, NHTSA has stated that .08 BAC laws have a general deterrent effect on drinking and driving among all drivers. Also, young drivers violating .08 BAC laws have been prosecuted under those laws without regard to age, suggesting that these laws do not affect only adults. For example, in California, 13,067 drivers under 21 were convicted under the state's .08 BAC law in 1997, compared with 11,517 drivers under 21 convicted under the state's "zero tolerance" BAC law. Finally, with the exception of the 1994 NHTSA staff study, all other studies of the effect of .08 BAC laws, including the recent 11-state and North Carolina studies, have included persons under 21 in their analyses.

Including persons under 21 years old would have changed these study results. In particular, the study would have found no statistically significant reductions associated with .08 BAC laws for drivers at low BAC levels. The findings regarding drivers at high BAC levels—a group that contains over 3 times as many drivers—would have remained substantially unchanged.

The study warns that "it is important to interpret estimates of lives saved due to any single law with considerable caution." In particular, as the study notes, factors such as public education, enforcement, and changes in societal norms and attitudes toward alcohol have produced long-term reductions in drunk driving deaths over many years. This study did more to control for extraneous factors than any of the other multistate studies, but this is inherently difficult to do, and in this case the authors estimate that 50 to 60 percent of the reductions in alcohol-related fatalities are explained by the laws it reviewed and the other factors it considered, a moderate level for statistical analyses of this type. Because of the uncertainties, the study's estimate of lives saved is also expressed as a range—and the number of lives saved in states with .08 BAC laws could have been as few as 88 or as many as 472.[11] Similarly, if the states without .08 BAC laws enacted them and experienced reductions comparable to those found in the study, the number of lives saved annually was projected to be as few as 200 or as

---

[11]The study made range estimates at the 95 percent confidence level, meaning that one would expect these results to occur in 95 out of 100 cases.

continues

Table 3: Drivers Involved in Fatal Crashes, 1995–97

	1995	1997	Difference
Alcohol-involved drivers	14,269	13,393	(6.1%)
Sober drivers	41,895	43,209	3.1%
All drivers	56,164	56,602	0.8%
Ratio of alcohol-involved drivers to sober drivers	34%	31%	(9%)

Source: GAO's analysis of FARS data.

many as 958. While the study reported results for the three laws it reviewed, including .08 BAC laws, the study also concluded that "the attribution of savings to any single law should be made with caution since each new law builds to some extent on existing legislation and on other ongoing trends and activities."

Conclusions

While indications are that .08 BAC laws in combination with other drunk driving laws as well as sustained public education and information efforts and strong enforcement can be effective, the evidence does not conclusively establish that .08 BAC laws by themselves result in reductions in the number and severity of crashes involving alcohol. Until recently, limited published evidence existed on the effectiveness of .08 BAC laws, and NHTSA's position—that this evidence was conclusive—was overstated. In 1999, more comprehensive studies have been published that show many positive results, and NHTSA's characterization of the results has been more balanced. Nevertheless, these studies fall short of providing conclusive evidence that .08 BAC laws by themselves have been responsible for reductions in fatal crashes.

Because a state enacting a .08 BAC law may or may not see a decline in alcohol-related fatalities, it is difficult to accurately predict how many lives would be saved if all states passed .08 BAC laws. The effect of a .08 BAC law depends on a number of factors, including the degree to which the law is publicized; how well it is enforced; other drunk driving laws in effect; and the unique culture of each state, particularly public attitudes concerning alcohol.

As drunk driving continues to claim the lives of thousands of Americans each year, governments at all levels seek solutions. Many states are considering enacting .08 BAC laws, and the Congress is considering requiring all states to enact these laws. Although a strong causal link between .08 BAC laws by themselves and reductions in traffic fatalities is absent, other evidence, including medical evidence on impairment, should be considered when evaluating the effectiveness of .08 BAC laws. A .08 BAC law can be an important component of a state's overall highway safety program, but a .08 BAC law alone is not a "silver bullet." Highway safety research shows that the best countermeasure against drunk driving is a combination of laws, sustained public education, and vigorous enforcement.

Agency Comments and Our Evaluation

DOT provided comments on a draft of this report . . . . The Department generally agreed with the information presented in the report. DOT reiterated its long-standing commitment to a systems approach for combating drunk driving and stated that while no individual component, including .08 BAC laws, is effective in isolation, the overall evidence supports the effectiveness of .08 BAC laws. DOT stated that the four original studies provided positive, if not conclusive, results and formed a reasonable basis for supporting .08 BAC laws. The three recent studies added to this body of evidence, including the North Carolina study, which, while finding little clear effect of the state's .08 BAC law, did find reductions. Consequently, DOT concluded that significant reductions have been found in most states, that consistent evidence exists that .08 BAC laws, at a minimum, add to the effectiveness of laws and activities already in place, and that a persuasive body of evidence is now available to support the Department's position on .08 BAC laws.

Overall, we believe that DOT's assessment of the effectiveness of .08 BAC laws is fairly consistent with our own. We agree with DOT on the importance of a systems approach to combating drunk driving; we have noted examples in this report such as the state of California, where .08 BAC laws were not effective until other complementary measures were put into place. DOT did not disagree with our discussion concerning the limitations and methodological concerns for three of the first four studies or with our assessment that recent studies reach difference conclusions about the effectiveness of .08 BAC laws; we believe those study results must be viewed in the context of their limitations and conclusions. Although DOT stated that studies showed significant reductions in most states, the 11-state study demonstrated reductions associated with .08 BAC laws in a minority of states (5 of 11) and a minority of the measures (9 of 33) it studied. In addition, many of the results DOT cited as consistent evidence supporting its position were reductions that study authors determined not to be statistically significant—thus, no conclusions on the effectiveness of .08 BAC laws can be drawn from them. Although we characterize the strength of the study results differently, we and DOT reach essentially the same conclusion regarding the effectiveness of .08 BAC laws, both by themselves and in combination with other measures.

Scope and Methodology

To determine the effect of .08 BAC laws on the number and severity of alcohol-related crashes, we analyzed the body of research published between 1991 and 1999. Of the seven studies, five were published by NHTSA, one by the state of California, and one by the American Journal of Public Health. We reviewed the studies' methodologies, findings, and conclusions and met with study authors at NHTSA, the Pacific Institute for Research and Evaluation, the California Department of Motor Vehicles, and Boston University's School of Public Health. We also discussed the studies and traffic safety issues with NHTSA officials in Washington, D.C., Boston, Massachusetts, and San Francisco, California; officials of the American Automobile Association, the Insurance Institute for Highway Safety, the National Sheriffs Association, Mothers Against Drunk Driving, the American Beverage Institute, the National Restaurant Association; and state traffic safety and law enforcement officials in California.

The scope of our study was limited to the effect of .08 BAC laws on the number and severity of alcohol-related crashes. We did not review several other arguments raised by both proponents and opponents of .08 BAC laws; for example, while we describe the medical evidence on impairment, we did not evaluate that evidence. In addition, our ability to review the severity of alcohol-related crashes was limited by the fact that the FARS database—used entirely by five of the seven studies and in part by a sixth—includes only fatal crashes. The .08 BAC laws reviewed may have had a greater or lesser effect on nonfatal crashes than it did on fatal crashes. Finally, section 2008 of the Transportation Equity Act for the 21st Century required us to review the effect of .02 BAC laws for drivers under 21 in reducing the number and severity of alcohol-related crashes. As agreed with your staff, we will not address those laws as all 50 states and the District of Columbia now have laws establishing BAC levels of .02 or less for drivers under 21 years of age.

continues

We performed our work from August 1998 through April 1999 in accordance with generally accepted government auditing standards.

We will send copies of this report to cognizant congressional committees; the Secretary of Transportation; and the Administrator, National Highway Traffic Safety Administration. We will make copies available to others upon request. If you have any questions regarding this report, please contact me at (202) 512-3650 or Ronald Stouffer at (202) 512-4416. . . .

Sincerely yours,

[Signed]

Phyllis F. Scheinberg
Associate Director,
    Transportation Issues

Transportation Bill Conference Driven By National Drunken Driving Standard, Limitation of Truckers' Road Hours

By Jeff Plungis

Two highway safety issues—a national standard for drunken driving and the number of hours truckers spend behind the wheel—are the focus of a House/Senate conference on the fiscal 2001 transportation appropriations bill.

Both were added to the Senate version of the bill (HR 4475—S Rept 106-309), and the debate is being driven by opposing interest groups.

The conference is expected to wind up in September. Both versions of the bill would provide $30.7 billion for federal highway programs. The House bill includes $15.8 billion for federal aviation, rail, maritime and safety programs; the Senate version, $15.3 billion.

The national standard for drunken driving is a favorite of Sen. Frank R. Lautenberg, D-N.J., who is retiring from Congress as ranking Democrat on the Transportation Appropriations Subcommittee. The Senate language would penalize states that fail to adopt a 0.08 percent blood alcohol content standard for drunken driving by taking away 5 percent to 10 percent of their federal highway grants.

Eighteen states and the District of Columbia have adopted the 0.08 percent standard for drunken driving. Nearly all other states have a 0.10 percent blood alcohol standard.

Lautenberg is backed by a coalition of safety groups, including Mothers Against Drunk Driving, Advocates for Highway and Auto Safety, Public Citizen and the National PTA.

The Clinton administration also has embraced the proposal.

The issue arose during debate over the 1998 surface transportation bill (PL 105-178). After lobbying by groups such as the National Beer Wholesalers Association, the National Restaurant Association and the Distilled Spirits Council, Congress adopted a compromise giving states incentives to move to the stricter standard, rather than threatening their highway funds. Only two states have adopted tougher standards since then.

Other opponents of Lautenberg's proposal include local and state government groups, highway contractors, and the American Automobile Association.

In a joint letter to lawmakers, the National Governors' Association, the National Conference of State Legislatures, the Council of State Governments, the National League of Cities and the National Association of Counties argued: "States and localities are on the cutting edge in the fight against drunk driving and do not feel that a one-size-fits-all approach can work to fight the drunk driving problem."

"Work zone safety is a serious problem for us, but we don't want highway funds used as a stick," said Peter Loughlin, a lobbyist for the Associated General Contractors of America.

Alcohol Industry Contributes

According to the Center for Responsive Politics, the alcohol industry has contributed $6 million in soft money, political action committee and individual contributions to candidates for Congress in the current election cycle, up one-third from the 1995-96 cycle. Anheuser-Busch Companies Inc. contributed more than $1 million of the total.

From *CQ Weekly*, Aug. 5, 2000.

continues

House Republican leaders have not stated a position on the issue. Speaker J. Dennis Hastert, R-Ill., received the fourth-highest total of campaign cash from the restaurant industry, according to the Center for Responsive Politics. House Transportation Appropriations Subcommittee Chairman Frank R. Wolf, R-Va.—an aggressive advocate of traffic safety—supports the Senate language.

Wolf's traffic safety work has put him in the forefront of debate on the other hot issue in the transportation conference: hours of service for truck drivers.

The Senate version of the bill would block the administration from promulgating regulations that would require longer rest periods for drivers but allow longer shifts at the wheel.

The death toll from truck accidents rose to a peak of 5,398 in 1997, but has eased slightly since then.

Last year, Congress passed legislation (PL 106-69) creating a Federal Motor Carrier Safety Administration within the Transportation Department—there had been a unit in the Federal Highway Administration—with the hope of bolstering government oversight.

But Congress sidestepped the question of how long truckers should be on the road. Safety advocates claim that fatigue is a factor in up to 30 percent of the fatal accidents involving trucks. The trucking industry says the figure is much lower, and that many fatal accidents are caused by reckless auto drivers.

Neither side likes the Transportation Department's proposal. Safety groups say it would allow truckers to drive up to 12 hours at a time, up from 10 under current rules. The trucking industry had been hoping for 14-hour shifts.

The industry also objects to the department's proposal to require "black box" data recorders that would monitor compliance with the rule, saying the boxes cost too much—about $500 a truck—and would be intrusive.

Trucking groups say they favor a negotiated rule-making process on hours of service. This is opposed by the safety groups, who say they do not have the financial resources to match the industry's legal firepower.

Advocates for Highway and Auto Safety vice president Jackie Gillan said a Transportation Department consultant determined the parties are too far apart for an effective negotiated rule-making. The level of public interest in the department's proposal indicates that the process is working the way it is intended, she said.

Drunken-Driving Plan Stirs Controversy

By Alan K. Ota

The Senate took aim at drunken drivers March 4 by passing a bill to withhold highway funding for states that do not set a blood-alcohol content limit of 0.08 percent by 2001.

With strong support from President Clinton, the Senate voted 62-32, with one member, John McCain, R-Ariz., voting present, to pass the bill, an amendment to the surface transportation reauthorization bill (S1173). The vote sets up a potential confrontation with the House, where opponents hope to defeat the measure by emphasizing Republicans promises to oppose unfunded mandates that cost the states millions to comply with federal regulations.

"It will save hundreds of lives each year," Clinton said on March 3. Supporters predicted that the standard would save 500 to 600 of the 17,000 people who die each year in traffic accidents related to alcohol.

McCain recused himself from the vote to avoid a perceived conflict of interest because his father-in-law owns a beer distributorship for Anheuser-Busch Co.

The Senate voted 43-56, with McCain voting present, on March 5 to defeat an amendment to bar sales of alcohol from drive-through outlets.

It voted 52-47, with McCain voting present, to pass an amendment to ban driving with an open alcoholic beverage container in the car, not necessarily drinking.

New Standard

The new blood-alcohol limit would put pressure on 33 states that have a blood-alcohol content limit of 0.10 for drunken-driving offenses and two states, Massachusetts and South Carolina, that do not use blood-alcohol content to prove intoxication.

Under the amendment, the government would withhold 5 percent of federal transportation funding from states that failed to adopt the standard by Oct. 1, 2001. Withholding would double to 10 percent annually in 2002.

House Transportation and Infrastructure Committee Chairman Bud Shuster, R-Pa., opposed the measure, calling it a "one-size-fits-all solution," and arguing for other incentives to encourage states to adopt the tougher standard.

Rep. Nita M. Lowey, D-N.Y., has sponsored a similar proposal (HR981) with more than 60 cosponsors. "The Senate victory has given us a big boost in the House," she said.

But Hank Dittmar, executive director of the Surface Transportation Policy Project, a nonprofit group that supports the measure and specializes in environmental and traffic safety issues, said the outcome in the House might be influenced by strong opposition to unfunded federal mandates, a plank in the House Republicans' "Contract with America" legislative agenda from the 1994 election.

"There has been an anti-regulatory fervor in Congress. And this vote seems to run against that," Dittmar said.

Indeed, the states' rights issues raised by Shuster, Senate Majority Leader Trent Lott, R-Miss., and other opponents of the bill echoed earlier debates over federal traffic safety rules. In 1995, the 104th Congress repealed federal highway speed limits and penalties on states that did not require motorcyclists to wear helmets as part of the National Highway System Designation Act (PL 104-59).

From *CQ Weekly*, March 7, 1998.

continues

Bipartisan Support

The new standard drew bipartisan support in the Senate, with senators on both sides speaking in favor of tougher laws to fight drunken driving.

Republican Strom Thurmond of South Carolina initially agreed to cosponsor the amendment but withdrew after studying its text and voted against it. "No matter how strict I feel laws regarding drunken driving should be, it is not the role or the responsibility of federal government to make state law," said Thurmond, whose 22-year-old daughter was killed by a drunken driver in 1993.

The restaurant and beer industries joined states' rights advocates in opposing the tougher standard, arguing that it would penalize social drinkers instead of heavy drinkers responsible for most accidents.

"This proposal simply punishes behavior that is not part of the drunk driving problem and distracts us from real solutions," said Rick Berman, general counsel of the American Beverage Institute, a trade association representing 5,000 restaurants that serve alcohol.

The liquor industry was divided, however. While beer-related businesses were in opposition, the Wine Institute and the Distilled Spirits Council, trade associations representing liquor distillers, took a neutral stance.

"We think it is an issue best dealt with by the states," said Bobby Koch, a spokesman for the Wine Institute. "We have not taken a position on the .08 federal standard."

The bill was backed up by a strong lobbying campaign by traffic safety advocates, including Mothers Against Drunk Driving (MADD), a group representing families of victims of traffic accidents involving drunken drivers.

Index

www.ingramcontent.com/pod-product-compliance
Lightning Source LLC
Chambersburg PA
CBHW080252030426
42334CB00023BA/2786